IOWA STATE UNIVERSITY LIBRARY

THE REFERENCE SHELF

Volume II Number 5

RESTRICTION OF IMMIGRATION

Compiled by
EDITH M. PHELPS

NEW YORK
THE H. W. WILSON COMPANY
1924

Published January 1924
Printed in the United States of America

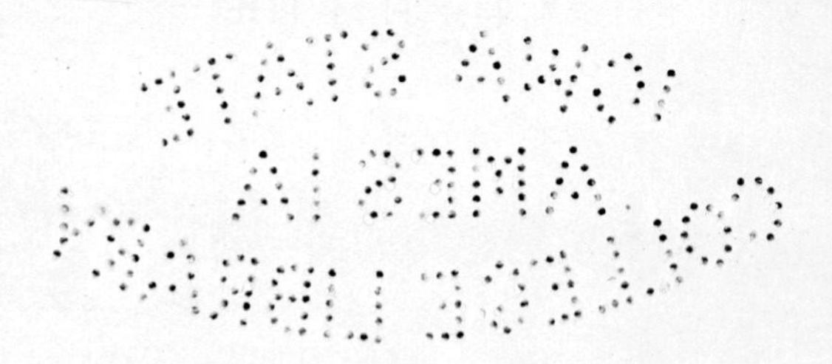

INTRODUCTION

One of the first bills to be introduced into the new Sixty-eighth Congress which convened December 3, 1923, is that prepared by the House Committee on Immigration and Naturalization which failed to pass the previous Congress. It was referred back to the committee which then announced public hearings on the bill to be held December 26-31.

It is necessary that Congress enact new legislation regulating immigration into the United States during this session since the present quota law expires by limitation on June 30, 1924. This law, passed in 1921 as a stop-gap until a permanent scientific measure could be prepared, was renewed for another year in default of Congress to pass the legislation desired. It is difficult to see how such legislation can be any longer deferred.

The proposed bill is, in fact, a revision of the quota law which has been doing service for the past three years. It would enact into permanent law the quota principle, recognizing that never again should the United States keep its doors open to everyone. Its main provisions are

1. The percentage (2 per cent) is based on the census figures of 1890 instead of 1910, thus still further restricting the proportion of immigrants from countries other than those of northern and western Europe. In order that this may not work undue injustice to the smaller nationalities, a minimum of four hundred immigrants is allowed to enter from any country.

2. Exceptions from the quota are to be made in the case of immediate relatives of those already here, and in the case of those who have been in America before and are returning from abroad.

3. Selection of immigrants abroad is provided for

in this bill by the proposal to issue consular certificates to each intending immigrant before he starts on his voyage. These certificates will be issued only up to the numbers allowed by the quotas. This does not do away with the inspection, medical and otherwise, at the United States port of entry, but will keep from starting on their journey most of those who would surely be excluded when they arrive. It would also prevent deportations because the quotas have been exceeded.

4. More careful examination and more humane treatment of arrivals are provided for by limiting the number entering in any one month to 10 per cent of the total quota, instead of 20 per cent as at present.

5. This bill would supplement and not be a substitute for the general immigration law of 1917 under which about thirty classes of aliens are excluded for various reasons.

Altho this bill failed to pass the previous session of Congress, it aroused considerable discussion in the public hearings that were held and in the press generally. This discussion is reflected in the following pages.

Similar to other issues of The Reference Shelf, this number contains briefs, a selected bibliography, and reprints of articles on both sides of the question of further restriction of immigration. The material is all recent, covering the period since the volume on Immigration in The Handbook Series was issued. Public sentiment in regard to immigration has changed considerably during the past few years, the economic issue now being foremost, and it is public opinion as it is reflected in the press today with which this volume deals.

EDITH M. PHELPS

January 3, 1924

BIBLIOGRAPHY

Articles starred (*) have been reprinted, wholly or in part, in this volume.

Bibliographies

Library of Congress. Brief list of references on immigration. 5p. (Typew. 35c.) D. 13, '20. Obtainable only thru the Public Affairs Information Service, 11 W. 40th St., New York.

Library of Congress. Brief list of recent references on immigration and the labor supply. 5p. (Typew. 35c.) Ja. 21, '21. Obtainable only thru the Public Affairs Information Service, 11 W. 40th St., New York.

Library of Congress. Brief list of references on recent immigration legislation in the United States. 7p. mim. F. 9, '23.

Phelps, Edith M. Immigration. (Handbook Series.) p. 19-40. o.p. H. W. Wilson Co. New York. 1920.

Survey. 48:79-80. Ap. 15, '22. Restricted immigration. Charles T. Bridgeman.

Texas. University. Suspension of immigration. E. D. Shurter and C. A. Gulick, eds. (Bul. no. 2146.) p. 5-8. Ag. 15, '21.

United States. Supt. of Doc. Immigration: naturalization, citizenship, Chinese, Japanese, Negroes, enlistment of aliens: list of publications for sale by the supt. of doc. (Price List 67, 6th ed.) 10p. N. '22.

General References

Books, Pamphlets and Documents

Beard, Annie E. S. Our foreign-born citizens. $2. Crowell. 1922.

A collection of life sketches of "foreign-born" citizens who have achieved things, Agassiz, Carnegie, Audubon, etc.

California Commonwealth Club Transactions. v. 18, No. 5. 191-250p. S. '23. Immigration restriction.

Claghorn, Kate Holliday. Immigrants' day in court. $2.50. Harper. New York. 1923.

p. 305-34. Court procedure relating to immigration laws and their enforcement.

Eliot, Charles W. What is an American? 6p. pa. National Liberal Immigration League. New York. 1921.

Reprinted from Collier's Weekly.

Great Britain. Foreign Office. Dispatch from H.M. Ambassador at Washington reporting on conditions at Ellis Island immigration station. (U.S. No. 2. 1923.) 12p. H. M. Stationery Office. London. 1923.

International Labour Office. Emigration and immigration: legislation and treaties. 439p. $1.25. Geneva. 1922.

A comparative study of existing legislation in regard to immigration.

International Labour Office. International emigration commission, Geneva, August, 1921. Report. 162p. Geneva. 1921.

Jenks, J. W. and Lauck, W. J. Immigration problem: a study of American immigration conditions and needs. 5th ed. rev. and enl. by R. D. Smith. 655p. $3. Funk and Wagnalls. New York. 1922.

Jones, Rosalie. American standard of living and world co-operation. p. 39-88. Cornhill Pub. Co. Boston. 1923.

Kellor, Frances. Federal administration and the alien: a supplement to Immigration and the future. 80p. 50c. Doran. New York. 1921.

Larkin, J. M. Our immigration policy and its social and economic effect. 5p. table. 25c. National Personnel Association. New York. 1922.

Laughlin, Harry H. Analysis of America's modern melting pot; hearings before the Committee on immigration and naturalization, House of representatives. November 21, 1922. Govt. Ptg. Office. Washington, D.C. 1923.

Lawrence, G. Alfred. Employment of intelligence tests in the control of immigration. pa. 143 W. 86th St. New York. 1922.

Memphis. Chamber of Commerce. Journal. 6:9-10. O. '23. Selective immigration: the right people for the right places; best solution of our development needs. C. E. Collins.

National Conference of Social Work. Proceedings. 1921: 453-65. Present immigration outlook. A. Sum and others.

National Conference of Social Work. Proceedings. 1922: 492-8. Immigration and the International labor organization.

National Industrial Conference Board. Immigration problem in the United States. (Research rept. No. 58.) 130p. tab. chart. $1.50. 10 E. 59th St. New York. 1923.

Very good. Recommended for purchase.

Panunzio, Constantine. Soul of an immigrant. $2. Macmillan. New York. 1921.

Phelps, Edith M. Immigration. (Handbook Series.) xi,370p. o.p. H. W. Wilson Co. New York. 1920.

Texas. University. Suspension of immigration. E. D. Shurter and C. A. Gulick, eds. (Bul. No. 2146.) 47p. Ag. 15, '21.

United States. Bureau of Immigration. Immigration laws: act of Feb. 5, 1917, and acts approved Oct. 16, 1918, Oct. 19, 1918, May 10, 1920, June 5, 1920, Dec. 26, 1920, and May 19, 1921; rules of May 1, 1917, sixth edition, Sep. 1921; amendments to rules 1, 4, 12, 13, 16, 22 and 31, and regulations under acts approved Dec. 26, 1920 and May 19, 1921. 118p. map. 1921.

Text of laws.

United States. House. Committee on Immigration and Naturalization. Admission of aliens in excess of percentage quotas for June: hearings June 10, 1921; statements of W. W. Husband and others. (U.S. 67th Cong., 1st sess.) serial 4. 79-128p. 1921. Apply to Congressman.

United States. House. Committee on Immigration and Naturalization. Admission of certain refugees from Near Eastern countries and restriction of immigration into the United States, including revision of the quota act: report. (U.S. 67th Cong., 4th sess. H. Rept. No. 1621.) 43p. 1923. Apply to Congressman.

United States. House. Committee on Immigration and Naturalization. Emergency immigration legislation: hearing before the committee on H.R. 14461, a bill to provide for the protection of the citizens of the United States by the temporary suspension of immigration, etc. (U.S. 66th Cong., 3d sess.) 713p. 1921. Apply to Congressman.

United States. House. Committee on Immigration and Naturalization. Emergency immigration legislation: hearings, April 15 and 26, 1921: report. [to accompany H.J. Res. 153.] (U.S. 67th Cong., 1st sess.) serial 2. 19-61p. 1921. Apply to Congressman.

United States. House. Committee on Immigration and Naturalization. Immigration and labor: hearings on H.R. 7826 and H.R. 11730. January 3-5, 22 and 24, 1923. (U.S. 67th Cong., 4th sess.) serial 5-c. 227-599p. 1923. Apply to Congressman.

United States. House. Committee on Immigration and Naturalization. Immigration for fiscal year, ended June 30, 1922: hearings, Aug. 22, 1922; statements of W. W. Husband and R. C. White. (U.S. 67th Cong., 2d sess.) serial 6-B. 593-625p. Aug. 22, 1922. Apply to Congressman.

United States. House. Committee on Immigration and Naturalization. Immigration: hearings, Dec. 13-20, 1921; Jan. 12, 21, 24 and 26, Feb. 9 and 13, 1922; etc. (U.S. 67th Cong., 2d sess.) serial 1-B. 504p. 1922. Apply to Congressman.

United States. House. Committee on Immigration and Naturalization. Operation of percentage immigration law for five months [June 3-Oct. 31, 1921]: hearings Nov. 10, 1921; statement of W. W. Husband. (U.S. 67th Cong., 1st sess.) serial 9. 981-1003p. 1921. Apply to Congressman.

United States. Laws, statutes, etc. Immigration laws. 7th ed. pa. 10c. Supt. of doc. Washington, D.C. 1922.

United States. Senate. Committee on Immigration. Amendment to immigration law: hearing on S. 4222, a bill to amend the act entitled "An act to limit the immigration of aliens into the United States," approved May 19, 1921, as amended and extended, Jan. 24, 1923. (U.S. 67th Cong., 4th sess.) 41p. 1923. Apply to Congressman.

Young, Kimball. Mental differences in certain immigrant groups. pa. $1. Univ. of Ore. 1922.

PERIODICALS

American Industries. 22:29-30. Jl. '22. Taking stock of the immigrant.

American Industries. 23:5-40. F. '23. Problem of our immigration; symposium.

*American Machinist. 58:393-5. Mr. 15, '23. Immigration—or machinery. K. H. Condit.

American Machinist. 59:220. Ag. 9, '23. Where do the immigrants go?

Annalist. 17:143-4. Ja. 24, '21. Seek equitable solution of our immigration problem. Sidney L. Gulick.

Annalist. 17:225-6. F. 21, '21. Immigration problem stripped of fear and hysteria. Frances Kellor.

Annalist. 22:392-3. S. 24, '23. Economic aspects of immigration. R. Estcourt.

*Annals of the American Academy. 107:56-62. My. '23. Canada's immigration policy. Robert J. C. Stead.

Commercial and Financial Chronicle. 112:2375-6. Je. 4, '21. Immigration bill signed by President Harding; text.

Congressional Digest. Jl.-Ag. '23.

This entire number is devoted to immigration and is recommended for first purchase. Publisher, Alice Gram Robinson, Munsey Bldg., Washington, D. C. 50c.

Congressional Record. N. 21, '21. Restriction of immigration: racial aspects. Madison Grant.

For limiting of immigration to those of Nordic strain.

Contemporary Review. 121:468-74. Ap. '22. America's new immigration policy. H. W. Horwill.

Current History Magazine, New York Times. 14:600-5. Jl. '21. Important facts regarding recent immigration Daniel C. Brewer.

Current History Magazine, New York Times. 15:604-9. Ja. '22. How restricted immigration works out. W. W. Husband.

Current History Magazine, New York Times. 16:115-17. Ap. '22. Our immigration problem. Etta V. Leighton.

*Current History Magazine, New York Times. 17:1009-16. Mr. '23. That international person, the emigrant. F. H. Rindge, Jr.

Engineering and Mining Journal-Press. 115:570. Mr. 31, '23. Immigration problem. Robert S. Lewis.

Engineering-News Record. 86:57-8. Ja. 13, '21. Status of immigration.

Factory. 30:285-7. Mr. '23. Immigration and the factory manager.

Symposium of arguments from all sides.

Farmer's Advocate. 58:41+. Ja. 11, '23. Hunt for immigrants in other lands.

A survey of foreign fields and a study of Canadian immigration methods.

Homiletic Review. 85:312-19. Ap. '23. Some racial factors in American life. K. D. Miller.

*Industrial Digest. 2:96-7+. F. '23. How immigration affects business.

International Labor Review. *See* current numbers for Notes on migration.

International Labour Review. 4: 537-62. D. '21. International emigration commission.

International Labour Review. 5: 113-18. Ja. '22. Regulation of immigration in the United States.

International Labour Review. 7: 515-40. Ap. '23. Migration movements throughout the world in 1913, 1920 and 1921.

*International Labour Review. 7: 755-70. My. '23. Notes on migration.

International Labour Review. 7: 933-47. Ja. '23. Migration statistics for 1922.

International Labour Review. 8: 414-36, 561-85. S.-O. '23. Migration: a general survey.

Iron Age. 111: 163-4. Ja. 11, '23. Strong support for selective immigration.

*Iron Age. 111: 1573. My. 31, '23. Keen interest in coming of immigrants. L. W. Moffett.

*Iron Trade Review. 71: 1339-43. N. 16, '22. Immigration issue stirs nation. E. C. Boehringer.

Iron Trade Review. 72: 173-4. Ja. 11, '23. Disregard need for immigrants.

Iron Trade Review. 72: 601-2. F. 22, '23. Threatens to cut alien quotas.

Labour Gazette (Canada). 22: 1286-8. D. '22. Immigration policy of the Dominion government: announcement to the press. Charles Stewart.

Honorable Charles Stewart is acting Minister of Immigration for the Canadian government.

Literary Digest. 69: 19-20+. My. 28, '21. Our foreign-language press on immigration.

Literary Digest. 73: 15. Ap. 22, '22. Is the melting-pot spilling the beans?

Literary Digest. 73: 46-9. My. 27, '22. Why, and how, Europe leaves home.

Literary Digest. 76:16. Mr. 17, '23. Bootleg styles in immigration.

Literary Digest. 77:9-11. My. 5, '23. Opening guns in the immigration fight.

Literary Digest. 77:26-7. My. 5, '23. Machinery to replace immigrants.

Literary Digest. 78:17-18. Jl. 7, '23. Terrors of Ellis Island.

Manchester Guardian Commercial Supplement. November 16, 1922. 10th number of series on Reconstruction in Europe.

p. 633-5. New immigration law of the United States. W. W. Husband.

p. 636-8. Emigration policies of the Chief European states. Frances Kellor.

p. 638-40. Italian emigration since the war. A. Cabrini.

p. 640-2. Czechoslovak emigration to America. Gustav Habrman.

p. 642-3. Effect of emigration on shipping prosperity. D. W. Caddick.

Methodist Review. 106:442-53. My. '23. Emigration crisis in Italy. B. M. Tipple.

Monthly Labor Review. *See* sections on Immigration in the monthly issues.

Monthly Labor Review. 14:1071-3. My. '22. Agreement on labor and emigration between Italy and Brazil.

Monthly Labor Review. 14:1262-5. Je. '22. Emigration law of Yugoslavia.

Monthly Labor Review. 15:415-17. Ag. '22. New Czecho-Slovak immigration law.

Monthly Labor Review. 15:697-8. S. '22. Canada's new immigration regulations.

Monthly Labor Review. 16:248-61. F. '23. Immigrant aid; legislative safeguards and activities of the Bureau of immigration. Mary T. Waggaman.

Monthly Labor Review. 16:669-73. Mr. '23. Emigration from Czechoslovakia, first quarter, 1922.

Nation's Business. 11:17-18. Ja. '23. How to let in the men we need. W. W. Husband.

Nation's Business. 11: 19-20. Ja. '23. Newcomer as a citizen. John W. O'Leary.

Nation's Business. 11: 19-21. Je. '23. Can we sort them at the gate? Vernon Kellogg.

*Nation's Business. 11: 26-8. Jl. '23. Immigration—a legislative point of view. Albert Johnson.

New Republic. 29: 270-1. F. 1, '22. Deported.

See also New Republic. 30: 52-3. Mr. 8, '22. Tragedy of the excess quota. E. Abbott.

North American Review. 214: 13-20. Jl. '21. Future immigration. Frances Kellor.

North American Review. 217: 769-84. Je. '23. Humanizing the immigration law. Frances Kellor.

Outlook. 128: 601-4. Ag. 17, '21. When liberty turns her back.

Outlook. 128: 606-9. Ag. 17, '21. How Canada handles the immigration problem. Robert J. C. Stead.

Outlook. 133: 181-3. Ja. 24, '23. Turning of the tide. Natalie de Bogory.

Outlook. 133: 245-6. F. 7, '23. Labor shortage and immigration.

Outlook. 134: 62. My. 23, '23. Stocking America with people.

Outlook. 134: 658-9. Ag. 29, '23. British advice for Ellis Island.

Printers' Ink. 114: 114-21. F. 10, '21. After the immigrant passes the Statue of Liberty. Frances Kellor.

Review of Reviews. 65: 509-16. My. '22. How the immigration laws are now working. James J. Davis.

Review of Reviews. 68: 193-9. Ag. '23. World migrations and American immigration. Judson C. Welliver.

Saturday Evening Post. 195: 25+. Jl. 7, '23. Ellis Island sob stories. Ernest Greenwood.

Saturday Evening Post. 196: 3-4+. S. 15, '23. America goes a-marketing. Marcus E. Ravage.

Scribner's Magazine. 72: 358-64. S. '22. Has the westward tide of peoples come to an end? Frederic C. Howe.

Successful Farming. 20: 5+. Ag. '23. Shall we let down the bar? O. N. Kile.
System. 43: 587-90. My. '23. Immigration and the labor supply. D. F. Garland.

Affirmative References

Books, Pamphlets and Documents

Burr, Clinton Stoddard. America's race heritage. $4.20. National Hist. Soc. New York. 1922.
California. Commonwealth Club. Transactions. v. 17. No. 8. 365-80p. O. '22. Immigration and population.
Davie, Maurice R. Constructive immigration policy. 46p. 60c. Yale Univ. Press. 1923.
Roberts, Kenneth L. Why Europe leaves home. 356p. $3. Bobbs Merrill. 1922.
Weiss, Feri F. Sieve: or, Revelations of the man mill. $2.50. Page. 1921.

Periodicals

American Federationist. 29: 818-27. N. '22. Immigration and America's safety. Oliver Hoyem.
American Federationist. 30: 489-93. Je. '23. Immigration? utilize first what we have. Samuel Gompers.
American Federationist. 30: 657-9. Ag. '23. America wants no wide-open immigration. Samuel Gompers.
American Federationist. 30: 914-19. N. '23. Immigration.
Collier's. 68: 9-10. S. 3, '21. Melting pot or dumping ground. George Creel.
Collier's. 69: 9-10. My. 6, '22. Close the gates! George Creel.
Collier's. 70: 23. D. 2, '22. Pilgrims of 1922. W. L. Whittlesey.
Collier's. 72: 6. Jl. 7, '23. Picking and choosing Americans. Parkhurst Whitney.
Country Gentleman. 86: 1-2. Mr. 19, '21. Slacker invasion. E. V. Wilcox.

Country Gentleman. 86:8-9+. My. 21, '21. Screening the alien chaff. John R. McMahon.

Country Gentleman. 88:3-4. F. 24, '23. Immigration goulash. E. V. Wilcox.

Current Opinion. 74:399-401. Ap. '23. Keep America "white."

Current Opinion. 74:652-4. Je. '23. Keep on guarding the gates.

Engineering and Mining Journal. 115:172, 260. Ja. 27, F. 10, '23. Immigration. T. A. Rickard.

*Forum. 70:1857-65. S. '23. Selective immigration. James John Davis.

Forum. 70:1983-9. O. '23. Is America too hospitable? Charlotte Perkins Gilman.

*Independent. 110:181-3. Mr. 17, '23. Immigration and the future American. S. J. Holmes.

Independent. 110:280. Ap. 28, '23. Letting down the bars.

Independent. 111:30. Ag. 4, '23. Desirable immigration.

*Industrial Management. 65:247-9. Ap. '23. Shall we let down the bars? C. Coapes Brinley.

Industrial Management. 65:321-3. Je. '23. Our labor shortage and immigration. James J. Davis.

Astracts. Current Opinion. February, 1923, p. 201-3.

Journal of Heredity. 12:319-25. Ag.-S. '21. Immigration and the three per cent restrictive law. Robert De C. Ward.

Literary Digest. 75:18-19. N. 18, '22. Cry for more immigration.

Management Engineering. 4:49-50. Ja. '23. Economist's support of restricted immigration. Henry R. Seager.

Manufacturers' News. 22:13+. D. 21, '22. Don't let down immigration bars. Edward A. Steiner.

Nation. 116:597-8. My. 23, '23. Coming lack of workers.

New Republic. 33:58-9. D. 13, '22. No immigrant flood.

*New Republic. 33:310-11. F. 14, '23. Uses of labor shortage.

New Republic. 35:248-9. Ag. 1, '23. Immigration and labor shortage.

North American Review. 213:598-607. My. '21. Present and future of immigration. Prescott F. Hall.

North American Review. 215:145-54. F. '22. William R. Thayer.

*North American Review. 218:325-33. S. '23. Selecting citizens. Cornelia James Cannon.

Outlook. 128:604-6. Ag. 17, '21. While the immigrant was still an emigrant. John Gleason O'Brien.

Outlook. 131:256-60. Je. 7, '22. Immigration and naturalization. James J. Davis.

Outlook. 134:311-13. Jl. 4, '23. Quota law. Ernest Greenwood.

*Overland. n.s. 79:27-9. F. '22. Menace of the open door. Fred L. Holmes.

Rural New Yorker. 80:184. F. 5, '21. Wants restricted immigration. H. Boyle.

Saturday Evening Post. 193:21-2. F. 12, '21. Plain remarks on immigration for plain Americans. Kenneth L. Roberts.

Saturday Evening Post. 193:3-4. Ap. 30, '21. Existence of an emergency. Kenneth L. Roberts.

Saturday Evening Post. 194:11+. Ja. 28, '22. Shutting the sea gates. Kenneth L. Roberts.

Saturday Evening Post. 194:22. Mr. 4, '22. America last.

Saturday Evening Post. 195:10-11+. Ag. 12, '22. Canada bars the gates. Kenneth L. Roberts.

Saturday Evening Post. 195:24. F. 24, '23. Do we want coolie labor?

Saturday Evening Post. 195:3-4+. Ap 28, '23. Lest we forget. Kenneth L. Roberts.

Saturday Evening Post. 195:18+. My. 5, '23. Checking the alien tide. Isaac F. Marcosson.

Saturday Evening Post. 196:8+. Jl. 28, '23. Immigration, progress and prosperity. Edward A. Filene.

Saturday Evening Post. 196:23+. Ag. 25, '23. Americans on guard. William T. Ellis.

Scientific Monthly. 15:313-19. O. '22. Some thoughts on immigration restriction. Robert De C. Ward.

Reprinted as Immigration Restriction League. Publication No. 77.

Scientific Monthly. 15:561-9. D. '22. What next in immigration legislation? Robert De C. Ward.

Scribner's Magazine. 69:352-9. Mr. '21. Some biological aspects of immigration. Edwin G. Conklin.

Scribner's Magazine. 72:364-7. S. '22. Immigration problem: a practical American solution. R. L. Garis.

Scribner's Magazine. 73:216-22. F. '23. Westward tide of peoples: reply to F. C. Howe. K. C. McIntosh.

*Spotlight. 8:16-17. O. '23. Congress and the immigration problem. Dora B. Haines.

*Survey. 47:209-10. My. 14, '21. Negro laborer and the immigrant. George E. Haynes.

Survey. 50:241-2. My. 15, '23. Winds of propaganda. Robert W. Bruère.

Textile World. 59:2889+. Ap. 30, '21. Restriction of immigration. Thomas N. Carver.

*World's Work. 46:121-5. Je. '23. Great fallacy of immigration.

World's Work. 46:633-7. O. '23. Immigration peril. French Strother.

Negative Reference

Books, Pamphlets and Documents

*Gavit, John Palmer. Americans by choice. 18p. pa. National Liberal Immigration League. New York. 1922.

Reprinted from Survey Graphic for March, 1922.

General Contractors Association. Bulletin. 12:16-17. My. '21. Hewers of wood and drawers of water: the effect of restricted immigration upon construction in industry. Roger O'Donnell.

General Contractors Association. Bulletin. 12:9-11. Je. '21. Locking the door and hiding the key: what the three per cent immigration law will really accomplish. Roger O'Donnell.

✓ Hourwich, Isaac A. Immigration and labor. 2d rev. ed. $6. Huebsch. New York. 1922.

National Association of Manufacturers. Proceedings, 1920:167-90. Immigration policy. Louis Marshall; Will immigration injure our industry or our labor? W. E. Edge.

Issued from Sec. Office, 30 Church St., New York.

✓ National Conference of Social Work. Proceedings, 1921: 308-12. Unemployment and the immigrant. Joseph Remenyi.

*National Conference of Social Work. Proceedings. 1922: 458-66. Immigration under the percentage limit law, with discussion. W. W. Husband, with comment by Edith Abbott.

National Conference on Immigration. Proceedings. pa. gratis. Inter-racial Council. 233 Broadway, New York City. April 7, 1920.

Philadelphia Chamber of Commerce. News Bulletin. 10: 5-6+. Mr. '23. Vital need for labor for American industries impels manufacturers to insist upon changes in immigration law to allow larger quotas. J. E. Edgerton.

PERIODICALS

*American Industries. 23:9-10. Ja. '23. Constructive immigration policy. James A. Emery.

American Industries. 23:34+. Jl. '23. Sources of our immigration. Alexander Grau Wandmayer.

American Journal of Sociology. 27:71-85. Jl. '21. Significance of immigration in American history. Arthur Meier Schlesinger.

American Machinist. 59:185. Ag. 2, '23. Our immigration needs. James A. Emery.

Commercial and Financial Chronicle. 116:557-8. F. 10, '23. Our restrictive immigration law and the shortage of common labor.

Concrete. 18:sup.47l. Mr. '21. Loss of alien laborers. W. H. Barr.

*Constructor. p. 12-13. N. '22. Will restrictive immigration throttle industry? R. C. Marshall, Jr.

Also in the Magazine of Wall Street for September 30, 1922. p. 818-19+.

Current History Magazine, New York Times. 13:405-8. Mr. '21. Constructive immigration policy.

Engineering News-Record. 90:11-13. Ja. 4, '23. Immigration as affecting the labor situation. Magnus W. Alexander.

Forum. 70:1866-70. S. '23. Immigration and industry. John Emmett Edgerton.

Iron Age. 110:717-18. S. 21, '22. Scarcity of common labor in industry. Acheson Smith.

Iron Age. 112:331-2. Ag. 9, '23. Why foreigners are needed in steel plants. George Walter.

Iron Age. 112:972. O. 11, '23. Immigration problem. F. C. Biggert, Jr.

Literary Digest. 76:14. F. 17, '23. To put up more immigration bars.

*Metal Industry. 21:70. F. '23. Immigration problem. William H. Barr.

Nation. 115:404. O. 18, '22. Cutting off our man-power.

New Republic. 30:93-4. Mr. 22, '22. Trouble for aliens.

Overland Monthly. n.s. 81:30-1. Ag. '23. Immigration—asset or liability? John Chetwood.

Saturday Evening Post. 195:6. F. 17, '23. Steve Tokacz; the contractor's point of view on immigration. R. G. Kirk.

For other references see the current issues of the Cumulative Book Index, Readers' Guide, Industrial Arts Index, bulletins of the Public Affairs Information Service, and other similar reference tools available in the library.

The following associations sometimes have literature to distribute on immigration:

Immigration Restriction League. Address J. H. Patten, 204 2d St., S.E. Washington, D.C.

National Committee for Constructive Immigration Legislation. Sidney L. Gulick, Sec., 105 East 22d St., New York City.

National Liberal Immigration League, 309 Broadway, New York City.

REPRINTS

A CENTURY OF IMMIGRATION[1]

From the close of the revolutionary war until the war of 1812 there was a considerable but unrecorded amount of immigration into the United States. It decreased during the war of 1812 and after the close of the war in 1815, increased to two hundred thousand in 1817, a large proportion of the arrivals being sturdy, industrious workers. Nearly all of these became permanent residents and helped to settle and develop the country, as many have since done, but in a proportion decreasing as the area of unsettled territory and of free lands for homesteading has decreased. Meantime larger and larger numbers have been employed in mills, shops and on the vast amount of construction work that required men by the hundreds and thousands and an increasing number have concentrated in the seaboard and other large cities. Many have been frankly migratory, remaining in this country only long enough to accumulate the desired amount of earnings which they have carried back to their native countries to invest.

In March, 1819, Federal legislation was enacted that regulated ship transportation of immigrants and provided for recording the number, age, sex and occupations of arriving emigrants. These records, since then much amplified, show that from 1819 until 1919 there have landed in this country 33,076,813 aliens—a number nearly equal to one-third of the present population of the United States, which has increased about ninety-seven million since 1819.

The great majority of the immigrants have been day

[1] Public Works. 49:347-8. October 9, 1920.

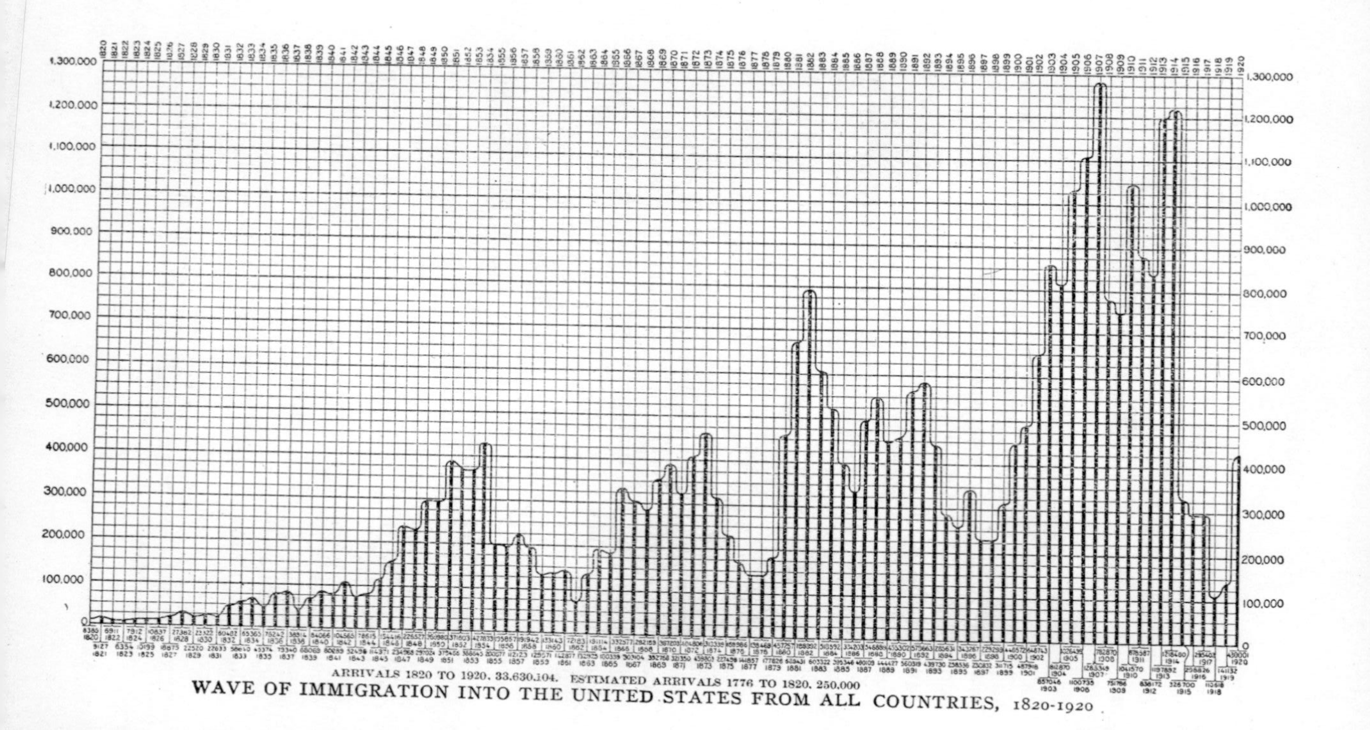

ARRIVALS 1820 TO 1920, 33,630,104. ESTIMATED ARRIVALS 1776 TO 1820, 250,000

WAVE OF IMMIGRATION INTO THE UNITED STATES FROM ALL COUNTRIES, 1820-1920

workers, common labor preponderating, with a goodly number of skilled laborers and artisans employed in special occupations and manufactures. They and their descendants have furnished a large proportion of the manual workers of this country, but in the degree, that they acquire citizenship and Americanization, their children enter into more skilled pursuits. With the great increase of productive and construction enterprises, more and more skilled and unskilled laborers are wanted, the demand exceeds the supply and increasing numbers of industrious immigrants are more and more necessary, especially in the present condition of world-wide demands for American products and the urgency of catching up with our deferred maintenance and extensions of all sorts.

The accompanying chart, prepared by the United States Bureau of Immigration, shows graphically the varying rates and exact amount of immigration for the century closing a few months after the end of the World War. For twenty-seven years, until 1845, the rate was fairly regular, increasing from 8,385 to 114,371. From 1845 until 1918, inclusive, there have been enormous fluctuations, producing four great waves, each with several crests, the major ones being in 1854 (427,833 arrivals), in 1873 (459,803), in 1882 (788,992), and 1907 (1,285,349 arrivals). These maximums were separated by extreme minimums of 72,183 in 1862, 138,469 in 1878, 229,299 in 1898, followed by a great drop to 110,618 in 1818.

Most of the variations are easily traceable to national conditions, which either forced people to leave their native countries or invited or repelled them here. The first wave was influenced by famine in Ireland and revolution in Germany. The next wave coincided with increased prosperity following our civil war; the third wave corresponded to a great shifting of the source of immigration from northern and western Europe to southern and eastern Europe, which furnished only 11 per cent in 1882 but 75 per cent in 1902. The fourth wave, 1901-1914, inclusive, is the greatest of all and corresponds with great prosperity and enormous construction in this country coincident with serious political, industrial and economic troubles and unrest abroad.

Sources of Immigrants

At first the great majority of immigrants came from Great Britain and Ireland; after 1820 increasing numbers came from Germany, until its maximum of 1882, followed by a decreased yearly rate of 17,000 to 40,000 from 1895 until 1914, when it almost ceased with the beginning of the World War, the total being much less than from Great Britain.

Italy and Russia were almost negligible until 1882. Since then both have increased steadily and enormously until almost obliterated in 1915 by the great war. Italy sent 32,160 in 1882, a maximum of 77,647 in 1903, and 29,391 in 1914. Russia was 21,590 in 1882, a maximum of about 291,000 in 1913, and 255,660 in 1914. Austria-Hungary was 27,935 in 1881, a maximum of 338,452 in 1907, and 278,152 in 1914. Scandinavia averaged approximately 50,000 per year from 1869 to 1914, with extremes of 11,274 in 1877 and 105,326 in 1882.

Summary of Arrivals from 1819 to 1919

Country	Total Immigration	Per cent of total
United Kingdom	8,205,675	24.7
Germany	5,494,539	16.6
Italy	4,100,740	12.4
Austria-Hungary	4,068,448	12.3
Russia	3,311,400	10.0
Scandinavia	2,134,414	6.4
Other countries	5,884,887	17.6

During the century more than 90 per cent of the immigrants came from Europe and 2.4 per cent from Asia.

The above data have been derived from the reports of the Commissioner General of Immigration, and are therefore authoritative.

RELATIVE PROPORTION OF OLD AND NEW IMMIGRATION GROUPS

Decades	Old Immigration United Kingdom, Germany, France, Belgium, Denmark, Netherlands, Switzerland, Sweden	New Immigration Austria, Hungary, Bulgaria, Greece, Czecho-Slovakia, Italy, Jugo-Slavia, Poland, Russia, Finland, Spain, Portugal, Romania, Turkey
1860-1870	98.4	1.6
1870-1880	91.6	8.4
1880-1890	80.2	19.8
1890-1900	48.4	51.6
1900-1910	23.3	76.7
1910-1920	22.8	77.2
1920-1922	36.8	63.2

CONGRESS AND THE IMMIGRATION PROBLEM[1]

The history of immigration and of immigration policy should be read in the light of the development of America from an unsubdued continent of forest and prairie and mountain to an agricultural and finally to an industrial nation. It was with the beginning of the change to industrialism that the quality and number of our immigrants began to change and that a real and tremendously significant "immigration problem" arose. That was in the latter 1880's and the 1890's. That period marked the turning of the tide from the so-called "old" immigration of desirable racial stocks to the "new" immigration from southern and eastern Europe. Yet the new condition was not understood by the country till the investigation of the United States Immigration Commission, which reported in 1911. Even yet there is no

[1] By Dora B. Haines. The Spotlight. October, 1923. p. 16-17.

adequate realization of the evil, and portent of still greater future evil, that has come to America through the failure to understand and heed what has been happening in the last thirty years of immigration. The flood of unrestricted immigration has already resulted in an alarming impairment of the average quality of the population and citizenship. The impairment which has occurred cannot now be undone, for it has entered into the life blood of the nation; but its vital significance demands the immediate attention of Congress to the end that from now on every foreign element that endangers American social and political ideals shall be rigidly debarred.

From the beginning of the country's history till 1882 there was no Federal regulation of immigration in any way. Such laws as were passed by states in which ports of entry for foreigners were located had practically no restrictive character. The policy of the nation was to encourage immigration by leaving it free and, by and large, this was a wise policy. The great area of the new country called for development. This call and the invitation of American social and political institutions met a response in kindred races and peoples from northern and western Europe who came in growing numbers to enter into the freedom and opportunity of this country. They were of Europe's best in fundamentally sound qualities adapted to America's needs. They were welcomed and became part of us.

The first Federal immigration law of 1882 went no further than to provide for the exclusion of convicts (except those convicted of political offences), of lunatics and idiots, and of persons likely to become a public charge. This policy was later gradually extended in a series of acts to cover the exclusion of polygamists, prostitutes and "white slavers," persons suffering from loathsome or dangerous contagious diseases, epileptics, alcoholists, and anarchists and advocates of violence.

A second policy, based on economic grounds rather than individual unfitness, was also entered upon in 1882, in the exclusion of Chinese laborers by treaty and by legislation, followed in 1907 by the exclusion of Japanese laborers in a similar way. Meantime in 1885 legislation forbidding importation of contract labor of any race was enacted, which was later developed in other acts and extended in an effort to exclude "induced" or "assisted" immigration.

Except for the beginnings of Oriental immigration, which were thus checked, there had been up to 1882 no special reason for considering restriction of the immigrant stream. Up to that time 11,547,570 immigrants had been admitted to the country and fully 95 per cent of them were of races that could readily be assimilated by our people—Anglo-Saxon and Celtic, Scandinavian, Teutonic, and in less numbers the French. Almost altogether the springs of the immigrant stream had been in the racial bloods of the north and west of Europe from the Scandinavian Peninsula to the Pyrenees.

But when our free public lands suitable for agriculture had largely been taken up and settled and when manufacturing began to develop on a greater scale to supply the market of a well populated country stretching from the Atlantic to the Pacific, the call of a growing industrialism was for an entirely different type of immigrant, and southern and eastern Europe began to respond to that call. By 1887 for the first time the proportion of the immigration from these southern and eastern European countries reached 25 per cent of the total from Europe for the year. By 1895, with the dawning of the era of the trusts, it was 42 per cent and in the next year jumped to 57 per cent. The McKinley, Roosevelt, and Taft administrations saw the proportion rise swiftly till in 1910 it was 81 per cent. Here within the space of twenty-five years was a tremendous reversal of the sources and quality and inspiration of our immigration. It coincided with and was undoubtedly caused by the increasing industrialization and trustification of our national life.

Meantime the number of aliens pouring in was mounting by leaps and bounds. From 1851 to 1880 the average number annually coming in was 261,000; from 1881 to 1892 it was 532,000; in the period from the panic of 1893 till the recovery from depression in 1899 the average fell again to just short of 300,000 a year. In the decade from 1901 to 1910 it leaped to 880,000 and in the four most prosperous industrial years of that decade the incoming tide was 1,113,538 souls a year. And of those from Europe practically eight out of every ten were Italians, Austro-Hungarians, Russians, Greeks and natives of other countries of southern and eastern Europe.

The Immigration Commission's report in 1911, after a large-scale investigation, pointed out the fact of this great reversal in the sources and quality of the new immigration, analyzed its dangers, and recommended "restriction as demanded by *economic, moral, and social* considerations." The methods of restriction suggested were various, including a literacy test, the quota principle, and the exclusion of unskilled laborers unaccompanied by their families; the reading and writing test being favored by a majority of the commission "as the most feasible single method of restricting undesirable immigration."

In response to this recommendation, Congress passed a bill incorporating the literacy test, but President Taft vetoed it. For four more years the gates stood open as wide as before, and in 1914, before the European war intervened to check and almost stop immigration, 1,218,480 aliens were admitted. Finally, in 1917, over the veto of President Wilson the literacy test was adopted, and when after the war the once more mounting numbers of immigrants had reached eight hundred thousand a year, 80 per cent of them from south and east Europe, the quota plan was temporarily enacted into law on May 19, 1921. It restricted immigration from the Old World countries to 3 per cent of the number of each nationality resident in the United States in 1910.

SALIENT POINTS OF THE 3 PER CENT ACT[1]

The number of aliens of any nationality who may be admitted in any fiscal year shall be limited to 3 per cent of the number of foreign born persons of such nationality resident in the United States as shown by the 1910 census. No more than 20 per cent of the annual quota of any nationality may be admitted in any one month.

Nationality is determined by country of birth, provision being made for population and quota adjustments in the case of countries whose boundaries have been changed since 1910. These adjustments are to be made by the secretaries of state, commerce and labor.

The act does not apply to government officials, their families or attendants; aliens in transit thru the United States; tourists, and aliens under eighteen who are the children of citizens of the United States.

These classes of aliens are counted against quota but may be admitted when the quota is exhausted: aliens returning from a visit abroad, aliens who are professional actors, artists, lecturers, singers, nurses, ministers, professors, aliens belonging to any recognized learned profession, and aliens who are servants.

Preference is given so far as possible to wives, parents, sisters, brothers, children under eighteen and fiances of (1) citizens of the United States, (2) aliens now in the United States who have applied for citizenship, (3) persons eligible for citizenship who served in government forces between April 6, 1917, and November 11, 1918, and who have an honorable discharge.

[1] From the Iron Trade Review. November 16, 1922. p. 1340.

The act was approved by the President on May 19, 1921, effective until June 30, 1922. On May 11, 1922, the President signed an extension which carries the act thru to June 30, 1924. The quota of admissibles in the fiscal year ended June 30, 1922 was 356,955, and in the year ended June 30, 1923, is 357,803.

IMMIGRATION AND EMIGRATION [1]

	1921-1922		and 1922-1923	
Immigrant aliens admitted......	309,556		522,919	
Non-immigrant aliens admitted.	122,949		150,487	
United States citizens admitted..	243,563		308,471	
Aliens debarred	13,731		20,619	
Total		689,799		1,002,496
Emigrant aliens departed......	198,712		81,450	
Non-emigrant aliens departed..	146,672		119,136	
United States citizens departed..	309,477		270,601	
Total		654,861		471,187
Net increase		34,938		531,309

IMMIGRATION INTO THE UNITED STATES UNDER THE QUOTA LAW [2]

Place of Birth	1921-1922 Quota 3% of 1910 census	1921-1922 Admitted	1922-1923 Quota 3% of 1910 census	1922-1923 Admitted	Quota 2% of 1890 Census
Albania	288	280	288	288	4[3]
Austria	7,451	4,797	7,451	7,358	1,103
Belgium	1,563	1,581	1,563	1,563	510
Bulgaria	302	301	302	295	61
Czechoslovakia	14,282	14,248	14,357	14,357	2,031
Danzig	301	85	301	263	228
Denmark	5,694	3,284	5,619	5,226	2,785
Finland	3,921	3,038	3,921	3,921	472
Fiume	71	18	71	67	11
France	5,729	4,343	5,729	5,034	3,914
Germany	68,059	19,053	67,607	49,258	51,227

[1] Figures taken from the Monthly Labor Review.

[2] Figures taken from the Monthly Labor Review and from Report No. 1621 of the House of Representatives (67th Congress, 4th Session).

[3] Each country will be allowed a basic quota of 400, making a possible total of immigrants, 168,201.

Place of Birth	1921-1922 Quota 3% of 1910 census	1921-1922 Admitted	1922-1923 Quota 3% of 1910 census	1922-1923 Admitted	Quota 2% of 1890 Census
Greece	3,294	3,447	3,294	3,294	47
Hungary	5,638	6,035	5,638	5,638	474
Iceland	......	......	75	59	37
Italy	42,057	42,149	42,057	42,057	3,912
Luxemburg	92	93	92	92	58
Netherlands	3,607	2,408	3,607	3,607	1,637
Norway	12,202	5,941	12,202	12,202	6,454
Poland (including Eastern Galicia)	25,827	26,129	31,146[1]	29,730	6,421[1]
Portugal (including Azores, Madeiras)	2,520	2,486	2,465	2,465	474
Rumania	7,419	7,429	7,419	7,419	638
Russia (including Siberia)	34,284	28,908	29,753[2]	28,619	2,843[2]
Spain	912	888	912	912	91
Sweden	20,042	8,766	20,042	19,867	9,561
Switzerland	3,752	3,723	3,752	3,752	2,082
United Kingdom	77,342	42,670	77,342	77,342	62,458
Yugoslavia	6,426	6,644	6,426	6,426	851
Other Europe	86	144	86	86	5
Armenia	1,589	1,574	230[3]	230	13[3]
Palestine	56	214	57	57	1
Syria	906	1,008	928	928	13
Turkey	656	1,096	2,388	2,388	129
Other Asia	81	528	81	81	45
Africa	122	195	122	122	44
Australia	279	279	279	279	120
New Zealand and Pacific Islands	80	88	80	80	42
Atlantic Islands	65	83	121	118	41
Total	356,995	243.953	357,803	355,480	160,937[4]

THAT INTERNATIONAL PERSON, THE EMIGRANT[5]

Our knowledge of emigrant peoples and countries is far too meager. We know that people have migrated since the beginning of history and will continue to mi-

[1] Including Pinsk Region.
[2] Including Bessarabian, Esthonian, Latvian, Lithuanian and Memel regions.
[3] Russian Armenia only.
[4] Each country will be allowed a basic total of 400, making a possible total of immigrants, 168,201.
[5] By Fred H. Rindge, Jr. The Current History Magazine, New York Times. March, 1923. p. 1009-16.

grate as long as there are conditions which push people out of some countries and attract them to others. Emigration and immigration are world problems, and not merely American ones. Nevertheless, as long as North America has three times the territory of Europe and the United States has one-third of all the world's wealth, we are sure to have immigrants. Over thirty million have come to us in the last hundred years. The smallest number arrived in 1823, only 6,354, and the largest in 1907, 1,285,349. This enormous figure was nearly equaled again in 1914 (1,218,480), and would probably have been surpassed this fiscal year had it not been for our restriction law.

This law has been passed again, with some improvements, for two years more, and the new annual maximum is 357,803. The number from each country is limited to 3 per cent of its foreign born in America in the census of 1910. Great Britain, Germany, Russia and Sweden did not nearly reach their assigned quotas last fiscal year, whereas a number of central and southeastern European countries passed their marks long before the fiscal year expired, on June 30. This clearly indicates one effect of the new law, namely, the reduction of immigration from central and southern Europe. These countries send only about one hundred and fifty-five thousand while the northern groups can send over two hundred thousand. In recent years the number of southeastern peoples remaining in the country has also been considerably less in proportion than the northwestern groups. In the case of several nationalities, a larger number of people have returned to the old country than have been accepted here. There are causes which evidently repel, as well as attract! The creation of new republics, the desire to see relatives, old homes, after the long war interval, and changing conditions in Europe have also attracted many back to the Old World.

After visiting twenty-three countries, one hundred

foreign cities, and thirty-six ports of embarkation to study this whole question, I realized that it is much more complicated than one imagines. The causes of emigration might be divided into two kinds—the "pushes" in countries of origin and the "pulls" in countries of destination. In the first group I discovered such causes as high birth rate, pressure for subsistence, lack of economic opportunity, high costs, burdens of taxation (so greatly increased since the war), religious persecution, political dissatisfaction, race subjugation, lack of educational opportunity, bad industrial conditions, fear of military service, class distinctions, social pressure and stimulation by returned emigrants, transportation agencies and prepaid tickets sent by friends already in America. Of course, war and the Peace Treaty have greatly modified these influences. For example, the Croatians and Slovenes, once oppressed by Austria-Hungary, are now a part of independent Jugoslavia; Lithuanians, Latvians, Esthonians and Finns have formed their own republics and are no longer connected with Russia; while the Czechs and the Slovaks are united in one of the most hopeful new countries of Europe. Thus there is less incentive for them to leave. As for the peoples of Austria and Bulgaria, they can barely gather enough money to emigrate. Germany has not nearly exhausted her assigned quota, and many Germans who came were obliged to pay about 45,000 marks for their third-class tickets ($10,530 at normal exchange).

The "pulls" in countries of destination include many conditions the reverse of those already indicated. The number of prepaid tickets sent by relatives in America has steadily increased, until it is a main attraction. The New World offers big money, large opportunity, free education and religion, marvelous recreation, true democracy, and a great adventure. This is a combination difficult to resist.

Two facts about recent immigration seem particularly

significant. Jews have furnished a larger contingent than any other race, and, as place of birth (real or supposed) determines nationality, they have entered America bearing passports from Poland, Rumania, Hungary and other countries. Their relatives in America have been more generous with funds and steamship tickets than the relatives of any other race, and efficient Jewish emigrant societies have assisted them in every possible way. One-fourth of all the Jews in the world are now in the United States. Another interesting result is that a larger proportion of recent emigrants have gone to the interior and to the farms. This is in spite of the well-known fact that very few Jews attempt farming. The other elements of the new immigration have been more active in this respect. This result was anticipated, inasmuch as the majority of our new immigrants have been of Nordic stock, and this group has always been less attracted to our crowded cities and industrial centers.

In the early days of lax immigration laws foreign nations shipped us large numbers of their undesirables. With few exceptions, this is not true today. Some countries have, however, granted passports to people of undesired races on condition that they would never return. In other cases, secret marks to the same effect have been stamped on passports. The people who earn and save for years to stake everything on their trip to America generally have sterling qualities. On the other hand, 80 per cent of our present immigrants need save little or nothing themselves, for their relatives in America provide the required passage money or tickets. These people are frequently undesirable. Their home countries do not send them to us, but their friends here bring them. This fact also largely determines their distribution, for they naturally go to those who sent for them, and that is generally in overcrowded centers. At present a number of European countries, like Sweden, prefer to keep their people at home. Other nations, like Italy, must send a fair proportion of their inhabitants abroad each year, for birth rates are high, economic opportunities limited and the safety valve may blow off. Italy has established over eight hundred schools for illiterates who desire to emigrate to the United States.

Most foreign governments today have well-managed emigration bureaus with carefully prepared policies. These bureaus not only assume great responsibilities for the welfare of their emigrants, but are prone to grant passports only to those who will worthily represent their mother country. The governments now look upon their emigrants as great economic and political assets, and therefore direct them to destinations where they may do themselves, and more especially their homelands, the most good. For this the mother-country can hardly be blamed, especially as emigrants in the United States send back over $600,000,000 in savings to Europe each year, in addition to their generous contributions for relief. Strenuous efforts are being made by some governments and their Consuls in the United States to hold the allegiance of their subjects, connect them with their own racial associations and societies, and encourage them to advance the interests of the mother-country in every way possible. Some nations even propose to give their subjects in America, whether citizens or not, a voice in the politics of the mother-country. In this divided allegiance there is grave danger for the United States, and the tendency is one to be understood and reckoned with.

The care with which some governments are directing emigration is illustrated by the new law in Czechoslovakia. Permission for transportation can be given only by the Ministry of Social Welfare, which reserves the right of control and inspection wherever transportation is managed. Agents of the emigration transportation business must personally guarantee and be responsible for all transactions made by their employees. They must keep their books in order and permit a survey of all business transacted in the transportation of emigrants. The agent may give transportation to the emigrant only on the basis of a written agreement, which includes clean food and lodging during the journey, and free medical attention. If the emigrant is not admitted to the country of destination, the transportation agent is obliged to provide free transportation to his last residence. Only steamships which strictly comply with the rules can carry emigrants. Special supervisors are authorized to see that the law is strictly observed, and are provided with free meals and transportation during both trips by the agent of the transporting office. There are many other careful provisions. Italy, Spain, Portugal, Poland and other countries also have elaborate laws governing the protection and welfare of their emigrants.

Recently an emigrant debarred at Ellis Island exclaimed: "When I get back I shall do everything I can to see that the bolsheviki destroy America." Yet there were good reasons why the authorities sent him back. Practically all who are debarred return with sorrow and resentment, and often to untold hardships. Home, possessions and money are gone. They are landed at a foreign port, and "home" may be several days' journey into the interior. This has led to frequent suggestions that all inspections now made at our ports of entry should be instituted at ports of embarkation, or, preferably, at our consulates in countries of origin. Canada has cordially received our emigrant inspectors in her midst for a dozen years, and the plan has met with considerable success. Several quiet experiments along this line are now being conducted by certain vice-consuls abroad. But the plan is fraught with great international difficulties. Most nations resent our seeming interference and the new power we might have over their subjects in the event of inspection at source. The plan will require a huge expenditure and trained men at every consulate. Moreover, the immigrants would require another physical examination at our port of entry, because they might contract contagious disease between Warsaw and Ellis Island!

It is significant that the International Emigration Commission, meeting in Geneva last August, passed a resolution calling for effective examination of emigrants at ports or frontiers, with the object of reducing chances of rejection by the country of immigration. These examinations would inquire as to whether emigrants had complied with all conditions stipulated by countries of origin and destination. Good beginnings have already been made in the examinations by some countries of origin before granting passports; in the inspections conducted by steamship officials, government doctors and United States health service representatives at most ports. But all this is a tremendous task, involving time. How great it is may be judged from the fact that in 1913, the last normal year, the Port of Bremen alone sent out over two hundred and thirty-nine thousand immigrants. There are at least fifty other important ports in Europe.

NOTES ON MIGRATION [1]

The Admission of Aliens to Great Britain

Under the Aliens' Order 1920 the Home Office has power, and has exercised it, to keep out of the country aliens who are thought to be superfluous to the needs of the country. No alien can land in Great Britain with a view to taking employment unless he has a permit from the Ministry of Labour, and such a permit is not given unless the Ministry of Labour is satisfied that there is no British man or woman available. With regard to the criticisms made by Labour members, the Home Secretary stated that there was no discrimination in the admin-

[1] From International Labour Review. May, 1923. p. 755-70.

istration of the act. He admitted that there were hard cases, such as separation of families where, for example, parents are aliens and were deported during or immediately after the war while the children are British-born. He considers, however, that these are inevitable, and that it is more important to consider whether the admission of such aliens would affect the employment of British subjects.

The Home Secretary gave the following preliminary statistics. The total number of aliens arriving in 1922 had been 316,159 (in 1921; 294,569), and the total number departing 315,765 (in 1921; 305,866); these numbers exclude persons in transit to another country. Of the arrivals 1,972 (859 men and 1,113 women) were admitted on a Ministry of Labour permit. In addition, 7,928 aliens were admitted who intended to remain for at least six months; they could not, however, be regarded as "alien immigrants." The remainder were travellers, etc. belonging to the non-immigrant classes. There were further on January 31, 1923 a total of 29,197 ex-enemy aliens living in Great Britain, including British-born wives and widows.

As regards the attitude of countries of immigration it is interesting to note that opinion in Argentina has lately been exercised as to the advisability of encouraging immigration. The press shows that there are two currents of opinion. On the one hand, it is argued that immigration is necessary to maintain population and to develop the resources of the country; on the other hand, opposition is expressed to the encouragement of an artificial migration movement to Argentina; thus several papers protest against the recent arrival of a certain number of Bulgarian families who, it is said, were tempted to emigrate by promises which it is impossible to carry into effect. Other papers stress the great advantage which would ensure if an active and systematic policy of immigration were pursued. They recommend that Argentina should send delegates to international conferences and should follow movements in the countries of emigration with great attention. Public opinion seems to be increasingly interested in the matter. No legislation has, however, yet been formulated, with the sole exception of several bills introduced by the government into Parliament at the beginning of February 1923 on the subject of home settlement.

In a report submitted to the Secretary of Labour of the Republic, the head of the National Employment Office (*Registro nacional de colocaciones*) drew attention to the balance sheet of the Banco di Napoli, which shows that over 46,000,000 lire were sent home by Italians in Argentina in 1922 (as against 35,855,000 in 1921). In his opinion seasonal immigration is chiefly responsible for this outflow of money, and tends to impoverish Argentina. The press, however, do not agree with this interpretation of the figures and the judgment was passed on seasonal immigration, stating that the productive work performed in Argentina by immigrants, whether permanent or seasonal, makes up to a very large extent for the savings they may send home.

In the Uruguayan Parliament a bill was introduced on January 23 by a group of deputies, the purpose of which is to amend the constitution so as to allow aliens to acquire Uruguayan nationality while at the same time retaining the nationality of their country of origin. In the report attached to the bill, it is stated that the number of immigrant aliens in Uruguay who acquire naturalisation rights might be very greatly increased if it could be arranged that they need not renounce their original nationality. Such a proposal amending the constitution would be in the national interest, inasmuch as it would considerably increase the size of the national electorate; it would also be of great advantage to immigrants, who would thus be able to enjoy the same opportunities of exercising their rights as is accorded to nationals of the Uruguayan Republic.

IMMIGRATION REGULATIONS[1]

The Canadian immigration regulations debar from Canada immigrants of the following classes:

1. Idiots, imbeciles, feeble-minded persons, epileptics, insane persons and persons who have been insane at any time previously.
2. Persons afflicted with tuberculosis or with any contagious or infectious disease.
3. Persons who are dumb, blind, or otherwise physically defective, unless security is given against such becoming a public charge in Canada.
4. Persons over fifteen years of age who are unable to read. Exception is made in the case of certain relatives.
5. Persons who are guilty of any crime involving moral turpitude; persons seeking entry to Canada for any immoral purpose.
6. Professional beggars, vagrants, and persons liable to become a public charge.
7. Persons suffering from chronic alcoholism or the drug habit, and persons of physical inferiority whose defect is likely to prevent them making their way in Canada.
8. Anarchists, agitators and persons who disbelieve in or are opposed to organized government or who advocate the unlawful destruction of property.
9. Persons who have been deported from Canada for any cause and persons who have been deported from any British dominion or from any allied country on account of an offence committed in connection with the war.
10. Immigrants who are nationals of Germany, Austria, Hungary, Bulgaria, or Turkey.

[1] From Canada's Immigration Policy by Robert J. C. Stead. Annals of the American Academy. May, 1923. p. 61.

Other restrictions also exist, or may be applied from time to time, particulars of which may be obtained by any intending immigrant from the nearest Canadian government agent. By an Order in Council at present (November, 1922) in effect the landing in Canada of any immigrant is prohibited except as hereinafter provided:

The Immigration Officer in Charge may admit any immigrant who otherwise complies with the provisions of the Immigration Act, if it is shown to his satisfaction that such immigrant is,—

1. A bona fide agriculturist entering Canada to farm and has sufficient means to begin farming in Canada.

2. A bona fide farm laborer entering Canada to follow that occupation and has reasonable assurance of employment.

3. A female domestic servant entering Canada to follow that occupation and has reasonable assurance of employment.

And provided further that the Immigration Officer in Charge may admit:

(a) The wife and family of any persons legally admitted to and resident in Canada who is in a position to receive and care for his dependents.

(b) The national of any country in regard to which there is in operation a special treaty or agreement or convention regulating immigration.

(c) Any British subject entering Canada directly or indirectly from Great Britain or Ireland, the United States of America or any self-governing British Dominion or Newfoundland, who shall satisfy the Immigration Officer in Charge at the port of entry that he has sufficient means to maintain himself until employment is secured.

(d) Any American citizen entering Canada from the United States, provided it is shown to the satisfaction of the Minister of Immigration and Colonization that his labor or service is required in Canada.

IMMIGRATION—PROPOSED 2 PER CENT LAW [1]

The present 3 per cent law expires on June 30, 1924. The question as to what shall take its place is vital to the United States and is one on which there should be clear and sane thinking. The great majority of our citizens are thoroughly convinced that there is imperative need, both of numerical limitation and also of much more careful selection. Yet a very wide diversity of opinion prevails as to the provisions which should be embodied in the new law.

Under these circumstances of confusion and contradiction, laymen wish to clarify their ideas on this matter. Therefore I have been asked to state the views of the majority of the House Committee on Immigration and Naturalization and to indicate what form forthcoming legislation is likely to take. During the session of Congress which ended on March 4 of this year, this committee of the House of Representatives made one of the most thorough studies of the whole immigration problem ever carried out in this country.

On February 15, after hearings at which every interest and point of view were represented, the committee reported an immigration bill which is thoroughly sound in its essential principles. By reason of the legislative congestion at the end of the session, no action was taken on this bill. While in some of its details this proposed legislation is not perfect, it does embody many excellent provisions. It is based on two essential and fundamental propositions: restriction and selection.

FIRST. The committee took a very important step in recommending a *permanent* percentage law and thus recognizing the principle that the United States should never keep its doors wide open.

[1] From article by Albert Johnson, Chairman of the House Committee on Immigration. The Nation's Business. July, 1923. p. 26-8.

SECOND. The percentage (2 per cent) is based on the census of 1890, instead of the census of 1910, as in the present law. The new measure thus aims to change the character of our future immigration by cutting down the number of aliens who can come from southern and eastern Europe. In other words, it is recognized that, on the whole, northern and western Europe furnish the best material for citizenship.

The provision for a per cent quota based on the 1890 census embodies a simple but practical solution of many of our immigration problems, based on historical facts. It would, so far as future immigration under the per cent provision is concerned, to a certain extent be automatically selective as well as numerically restrictive.

THIRD. The committee has taken another necessary step in providing for a better selection, with the established quotas, of the incoming aliens. This is a much-needed reform, which will heartily commend itself to everyone who is at all familiar with existing conditions. It is urged, again and again, that the present percentage law does not select; it merely restricts numbers. This is, to a large extent, true. The committee proposes a plan for consular certificates to be issued to each intending immigrant before he starts on his voyage. This certificate is to contain answers to questions essentially the same as are asked of the immigrant on his arrival at our ports, as well as full information about his health, civic record, political activities and character. It is to be verified by oath before a United States consular officer abroad.

Certificates are to be issued only up to the numbers allowed by the quotas. This would prevent the present hardships which result when aliens arrive here in excess of the quotas and must be deported.

Under this proposed plan, the real inspection, medical and otherwise, would be made at our own ports, as it should be, but most of the aliens who would be excluded on examination here would never start on their journey.

The certificate plan, then, would through the preliminary selection overseas, benefit the United States. It would also very greatly diminish the hardships of the alien. It is selective, and it is humane.

FOURTH. Another step looking toward a more thorough examination—general, mental and physical—of arriving aliens is taken in the provision that not more than 10 per cent of the annual quota of each nationality shall enter per month, instead of 20 per cent as at present. As things now stand, there is a tremendous rush to get in as soon as possible, and many quotas are exhausted before the year is half over. This inevitably means hurried and unsatisfactory examinations. If the quotas were spread over the year, the important work of medical and general inspection could be done in a far more leisurely and therefore in a far more effective way.

The foregoing are the provisions of the proposed legislation in so far as (1) definite numerical limitation and (2) selection within this limitation are concerned. The bill also embodies certain other provisions, the most important of which deserve mention here. The natural desire of our recent immigrants to have their relatives join them, thus relieving the hardship of dividing alien families, is recognized in the establishment of a very considerable group of immigrants who would be admissible without being counted as part of the quota. Those who have been in America and are returning would not be debarred, nor would immediate relatives of naturalized citizens and of those who have declared their intention of becoming citizens.

While the number admissible under the proposed 2 per cent quotas would be much smaller than the numbers admissible under the 3 per cent law, the very numerous exceptions in the case of immediate relatives would, without doubt, far more than offset this percentage reduction, and would permit the immigration of "refugees" who have near relatives in the United States.

It is probable that the number of relatives will be limited to a small percentage, as a safeguard against fraud. The provision for the admission of relatives should be made only for the relatives of citizens, who must in all cases be eligible under our general immigration laws.

The bill further provides that all nations shall have a minimum quota of four hundred eligible to enter the United States before the 2 per cent quota is applied, would not operate against immigration from Canada, Newfoundland, Mexico, Cuba and Central and South America, provided those seeking admission had been resident in those countries for five years, and permits the immigration of skilled labor outside the quota limits, "if labor of like kind unemployed cannot be found in this country," the question of the necessity of importing such labor to be determined in advance by the Secretary of Labor.

Thus far the new legislation proposed by the House Committee is a thoroughly constructive, logical and practical immigration bill. Its enactment into law would go a long way in "solving" many of our present immigration "problems."

This proposed new legislation would, it must be clearly understood, be in addition to, and not a substitute for, our present general immigration law of 1917, under which some thirty classes of aliens who are physically or mentally diseased, or otherwise morally or economically undesirable, are excluded.

IMMIGRATION AND THE FUTURE AMERICAN [1]

The last few years have witnessed a striking change in the prevailing sentiment of the American people on the subject of immigration. It has only recently come home to us that we are suffering from an attack of acute

[1] By S. J. Holmes, Professor of Zoology and Genetics, University of California. The Independent. March 17, 1923. p. 181-3.

indigestion. Immigrants have been pouring in upon us more rapidly than they can be assimilated. Much of this influx assimilates with difficulty—in fact scarcely at all in the first generation. Instead of the English, Scotch, Irish, Germans, and Scandinavians who made up the bulk of our immigration before 1880, we have been receiving hordes of Poles, southern Italians, Greeks, Russians, especially Russian Jews, Hungarians, Slovaks, and other southern Europeans—stocks less closely related to us by blood than the northern Europeans and less readily imbued with the spirit of our institutions. Our immigrants lodge chiefly in cities, forming little communities speaking their own language, and preserving, so far as possible, their customs and traditions. They show a very high percentage of illiteracy and they furnish a great part of the unskilled labor of our mines, factories, and streets.

Undoubtedly, the immigrant is an economic asset to the country. His labor adds to the wealth of those who employ him and increases the total wealth of the nation. On the other hand, he may impoverish those who have to compete with his labor. He takes the job of the native American, and the native American goes elsewhere, often, fortunately for himself, into a better position. The big financial interests of the country have very naturally been in favor of abundant immigration. The steamship and railroad companies want passengers; the mining and manufacturing companies want cheap labor. Immigration has been encouraged because, it is claimed, the resources of the country needed to be developed. There were railroads to be built, forests to be cut down and virgin soil to be tilled. The average American likes to see things go ahead. He is fond of bigness of all kinds and he likes to brag about it. Immigration, moreover, makes business, and business, it goes without saying, is a good thing to increase.

But in addition to the economic motives for encouraging immigration the Americans have been actuated by a more generous desire to extend to the down-trodden workers of the Old World the blessings of freedom and opportunity which this country affords. The average American used to believe that he lived under the most glorious government that ever existed under the sun. He felt himself a prophet of liberty. He would like to see his own political institutions replace the effete monarchies of less progressive nations, but in lieu of this, he would hospitably open the gates of his own country to the oppressed of other lands.

But the attitude of the average American is changing. He is suffering from an overdose of the unassimilated foreigner. He is finding that the foreigner creates many difficult problems and aggravates many existing evils. And with our increased growth of foreign populations he is finding that political power in many localities is passing out of his hands into those of aliens whom he has but very imperfectly indoctrinated with the ideas and ideals of American democracy. With continued influx of immigration at the pre-war rate and especially at the more rapid rate that would occur were no restrictions placed upon it, the American is beginning to wonder how long American traditions will last. Good old Puritan Massachusetts, which is no longer Puritan, by the way, but Roman Catholic, has, according to the 1920 census, 28 per cent of foreign-born population, and but 31.9 per cent of native born of native parentage. Immigrants and the first generation of their children make up over two-thirds of her population. New York city, which is the largest Italian city and the largest Jewish city in the world, to say nothing of being the largest negro city, has only 20.7 per cent of native born population of native parentage. We have hitherto gone on the theory that, however ignorant the foreigner must be, whatever may have been the institutions under which he lived, or whatever the stock from which he was derived, he or at least his children would become thorougly Americanized in time. We had counted on America changing the foreigner instead of the foreigner changing America. The latter possibility is coming now to loom up in a portentous manner. Of late years we have made frantic efforts at Americanization. The process we found had been taking place much more slowly than we should like, and we went out of our way as never before to hasten it along. No nation can be a great nation without a spirit of unity—a certain degree of like-mindedness among its people. It is desirable also that it contains much diversity, but it should be diversity on approximately the same level. An infiltration of a moderate number of people from other countries is a wholesome influence in counteracting the tendency to fixity which is a natural proclivity of social groups. But carried too far it would result in making a people a mere hodge-podge of heterogeneous elements.

Quite aside from the native quality of our immigrants there is a danger in admitting them in such numbers as seriously to disturb the economic and social stability of the communities in which they come to live. If we were to receive the millions in Europe who, we are told, are ready and anxious to emigrate to America, we should have such an overwhelming mass of ignorant, poverty-stricken humanity on our hands that "Americanization" in any reasonable time would be a hopeless task. Conditions in our cities are bad enough now. With unrestricted immigration they would become almost intolerable.

The greatest permanent danger, however, lies in the likelihood of receiving stocks of inferior inheritance. The American is beginning to suspect that some of our racial immigration is of low racial value. Just as there are families on a low mental level, so there may be peoples on a low mental level. Unquestionably we have been getting much of this kind of human material. Our laws forbid the entrance of the insane, epileptic, and feeble-minded, but we detect only the most obvious cases. At the pre-war rate of more than a million immigrants a year only the most cursory examination was possible with existing facilities. Consequently many undesirables slipped through only to find their way later into poorhouses or asylums for the insane, or otherwise prove themselves burdens on the community.

Immigration has been and may be again probably the most potent factor in determining the quality of the future population of this country. If it is to be regulated in the interests of posterity the task should be begun as soon as possible, even though, through lack of knowledge, we may come far short of regulating it in the proper way. We cannot afford to wait until we have all the facts in our hands before taking action. Several writers in dealing with this problem have advocated what I should describe as a misplaced caution. Professor J. W. Jenks, after commenting on the complexities and difficulties of the problem and urging a study of it in an impartial spirit, tells us: "When the facts are clearly established, we have then to answer the further question whether we shall admit or exclude or make a distinction among the races. Whatever the decision may be, we have the extremely difficult question of how we can make legislation and enforce legislation that shall do justice to all and inflict no needless suffering."

The quotation reveals, I think, an entirely wrong attitude. The writer implies that other peoples have a sort of vested right to come here and that we have to act very carefully and gingerly about excluding anyone desiring to enter. Why should we assume the burden of proof that certain stocks will make undesirable additions to our population? We may need twenty years of meticulous investigation before we can prove our case to the satisfaction of critically minded judges. In the meantime these questionable stocks will be pouring in upon us. Why not shift the burden of proof to the other fellow and require some assurance of his desirable qualities before admitting him to the country? We do not encourage people to enter our homes because we cannot prove that they are *not* criminals or imbeciles. We generally have some grounds for believing that they are at least respectable before we take them in. In regard to the immigrant the question should be not who can be proven bad enough to be sent away, but who can prove himself good enough to be admitted. The basis for selecting immigrants should be positive, not negative.

In dealing with the admission of aliens we should assume that immigration is not a right, but a privilege, and that we are under no obligations whatever to extend it to all peoples even of the white race. We may be loth to make invidious distinctions between different nationalities, but no foreign people has any more basis for objecting to such discrimination than some of our neighbors have for not being invited to our parties. In our 3 per cent rule we are now making discriminations, but it is under the cloak of a general mode of procedure. The proper regulation of immigration would probably compel us to abandon all pretence to impartiality and frankly state that there are several peoples that we do not want. If we should strongly suspect that the immigrants from any country are deleterious to our welfare, either socially or racially, we should take measures to debar them and revise whatever agreements on immigration we have made with the countries concerned. Whether these countries like it or not is a very secondary consideration compared with the preservation of the worth of our own future population.

It may, however, be unnecessary to undertake the delicate task of discriminating against peoples or nations as such. There is a growing consensus of opinion among unbiased students of the problem that we should have higher standards of admission. We let in altogether too many who are mentally below par. Our literacy test could well be made more than the very meager requirements that it now is. It would undoubtedly help matters greatly if all incomers were compelled to undergo a series of thorough mental tests given in the language of the persons examined. Despite present defects in the art of mental testing and despite an occasional injustice to the immigrant, a test designed to exclude everyone up to and including the level of a high grade moron would insure a much better result than we are now getting. Of course more thorough examination would involve great additional expense, but this would be a relatively small item compared with the gains from a more carefully selected immigrant population.

Australia, New Zealand, and Canada have regulated their immigration much more wisely than we, and consequently they are not suffering from some of the embarrassments with which we have to contend. We may well follow their example in many respects. As Mr. Roosevelt said, we want immigrants of the right kind, and it might even pay us to import them and give them a bonus for coming besides. We need good, healthy, intelligent, and enterprising stocks, provided that they do not come too fast for proper assimilation, and we could well afford to put up with considerable difficulty in getting them assimilated. But to import poor human material for cheap labor is not only bad economic policy in the long run, but a crime against future generations. In our over-emphasis of money getting and our neglect of the human values of our people we are in danger of selling our birthright for a mess of pottage.

Every American who is ambitious to see his country a truly great nation should be guided in his attitude toward immigration neither by considerations of wealth to be derived from imported cheap labor nor by a sentimental desire to make this country an asylum for the oppressed of other lands, but by the ideal of an America, peopled by strong, healthy, and intelligent men and women having the normal and wholesome instincts that make for sound character and harmonious social life. It is no charity to extend the opportunities of living here to the failures of the Old World. A policy of free admission would rather be a crime against the future children of our own land, for these have their rights as well as our contemporaries. It is to our descendants that we owe our first obligation. No misguided sympathy for the unfortunate inhabitants of other countries should ever permit us to jeopardize the welfare of our future population.

MENACE OF THE OPEN DOOR [1]

"What is the greatest problem in the social life of America today?" was asked Professor Ross.

"The thing that causes the most forboding to me is how to preserve democracy and popular government in a people that has become so heterogeneous as ours," said Professor Ross.

Roughly speaking moral and economic standards will be realized and new laws will be enforced when 80 to 85 per cent of the people are behind them. Now within thirty years it has become difficult to get that proportion of us behind anything whatever. There have come among us in the last half century more than twenty million European immigrants with all manner of mental background, many of them having traditions which will no more blend with American traditions than oil will blend with water. The people have become so unlike minded that you cannot get 80 per cent of them to back any advanced step. Suppose in England today we introduced millions of English of the age of Queen Anne, millions of the people of the time of Elizabeth, millions of the peasantry of the reign of Henry VIII. Would

[1] Statement of Professor E. A. Ross. Overland Monthly. February, 1922. p. 27-9.

public opinion and community policy in England be able to develop as they do today?

Yet this is the equivalent of what is upon us. Among us have come millions who have never acquired the habit of looking to sheriffs and courts for protection, but have put their trust in the "Vendetta" and secret societies, the result being that in certain of our cities American justice is quite foiled. Immigrants are in our midst who are entirely unprepared to accept our American policy of the total separation of church and state. Within a generation after our people generally have been brought to acknowledge the concern of the community in education, we were flooded with people from eastern and southern Europe who insist that it is a parent's prerogative to determine whether or not his child shall have any education and whatever education there is shall be controlled by the church and not by the state.

Likewise many have come among us lacking the American respect for women and this is one reason why we have so little success in the supression of the vilest forms of vice. In the course of the middle third of the 19th century a large number of the American people had been brought to look upon alcoholic beverages as a race menace. Then were introduced into our midst myriads quite innocent as to the perils that lay in the cheering bowl so that temperance was balked and the struggle against alcohol took on the form of legal prohibition. As a result of this growing heterogeneity society can scarcely make up its mind any more save on matters of such elemental appeal as fire protection, sanctity of property, good roads and public improvements. The "interests," politicians, and the foreign nationalistic organizations play one element off against another so that we are not getting on as we should.

Long ago Americans formed the habit of expecting their country to lead the world in popular progress. But we have had the mortification of seeing people after people pass ahead of us in such matters as education, status of women, sanitation, law enforcement, vice suppression, public morals, etc. Not only New Zealand and Australia, but the Scandinavian countries, and, in some respects, England have made strides that in many of our commonwealths we have been unable to make. Thus I noticed lately that in infant saving thirteen peoples are ahead of us. Such stalling and fumbling is the inevitable result of the cross purposes and confusion of ideas that result from excessive heterogeneity.

This is why I regard our persistence in the open door policy in respect to immigration as the greatest mistake the American people have made in our time.

SELECTIVE IMMIGRATION [1]

Few of us stop to consider that the United States during the past hundred and thirty years has been the goal of the greatest movement of people that the world has ever known. Of all the great migrations of history none has ever approached in volume the vast flood that has come to America since our forefathers founded here a nation based on human rights. More foreigners have passed through Ellis Island within a few months than there were in the hosts of the Huns and Vandals who destroyed the boasted civilization of the Roman Empire. The historians and scientists tell me that all the great civilizations of the past have fallen, not through hostile invasion, but through the peaceful penetration of alien peoples, usually entering their gates as workers or slaves.

The flood of immigration which has unceasingly rolled to this rich new land since 1790 has brought here a total of some thirty million of the older peoples of the world. One-third of the migration has come to us since 1890. The character of this continuous flood of aliens has

[1] By James J. Davis, Secretary of Labor. The Forum. September, 1923. p. 1857-65.

totally changed in the past two or three decades. Before 1890 the foreigners who came to us from Europe came from the northern nations; from the British Isles, the Scandinavian countries, Holland, and Germany. They were largely homologous with the original founders of the United States. The tide from northern Europe has halted and the bulk of the arrivals are from those nations of southeastern Europe and the Mediterranean shores which, with few exceptions have for centuries been the scene of much of the world's discord and strife and bloodshed. Some come from lands where oppression has bred disrespect for all government and disregard for all law. They come, not to face the dangers of a new and untried country, but to gain the ease and plenty offered by the greatest nation of modern times.

The aliens coming to us today raise many problems. Some of them come from the war-torn, or revolutionary countries of Europe, imbued with wild theories of political cure-alls, ready to preach the downfall of American principles and the destruction of all governmental institions. Others, though tainted blood, weak mentality, or physical fault, threaten the whole physical, mental and moral level of the American people.

There are many schools of though on this subject. I am no pessimist with regard to the future of the United States. I have confidence in the genius of the American people to meet this problem as they have met other problems of the past. One group in America today proposes to let down all bars against foreigners coming here. This group clamors emptily about America as a refuge for all the world's oppressed. In the cant of the enthusiast they picture this country as a sort of world hospital or ambulance. This group has as many subdivisions as there are alien races represented in the United States.

There is another group of men who have devoted much thought and study to the subject, who take the position that the immigrant is an unnecessary evil, and this group would bar all aliens except such elements as will strengthen the native human stock already here. These students hold that the laws of population and of natural fecundity operate to prevent an actual increase in our population through immigration. They say that population will increase just as rapidly if we bar out immigrants and allow the birthrate to provide our additional men and women.

Many of our public men support the form of restriction imposed under the present law which admits to the United States annually only as many representatives of foreign nationality as equal 3 per cent of the number of that nationality that was in the United States in 1910. This plan operated in the last fiscal year to restrict those coming from southern and eastern Europe, who had completely filled their allotted quotas. Northern and western Europe,—source of the so-called Nordic immigration,—in that year failed to fill their quotas, some of those countries sending here less than 50 per cent of their allotments. This year, it seems that the quota law is having the effect of increasing the percentage of aliens from northern and western Europe in our total immigration. Many of those countries will this year fill their quotas.

Now, there are also some among us who would absolutely bar all foreigners from the United States on economic grounds. They hold that an influx of foreigners which would give to us a constantly increasing supply of labor would tend to encourage industrial inflation, and, therefore, they would restrict production by restricting any foreign labor supply. For some reason there seem to be widely-differing viewpoints between the employers who manage our industry and the men whose labor makes our industrial system possible. To me this seems to be an utterly fallacious line of division, for I am daily more convinced that the cause of labor in America is the cause of industry in America, and that the cause of industry is the cause of labor. They must stand or fall together. If industry fails, labor must fail. If the employer succeed, the worker must succeed. If one die, both must die.

But I look at our immigration problem not from the standpoint of American labor alone, nor of the American employer alone, but from the standpoint of all America. This problem must be met by deciding what is best for us all,—what is best for our republic today and in the future. I am firm in the conviction that what is best for America as a whole is best for American labor and American industry.

Our immigration laws are far from perfect. They have developed in a haphazard way, influenced, in many instances by momentary expediency and by international considerations which, at times, seemed vital. One instance of this is our contract labor law. Years ago an employer could hire workmen abroad and bring them to their jobs in America. This system was abused and men were imported to work at lower wages than the established scales. Men were imported to take the places of strikers and in other ways the system was operated to oppress and exploit the immigrant. The pendulum swung the other way, and today our contract labor law is so stringent that a man in America cannot write to his brother abroad telling him of an opportunity of employment without rendering that brother inadmissible. This is going too far, for some of our best immigrants in the past have come from just such family connection as that. Today the immigrant coming to this country must come absolutely of his own volition, without financial aid, without asking for assurance of employment before he leaves his native land. He must risk his all and gamble on the prospect of finding remunerative work when he reaches America; and, for a man with a family, that risk is great.

Another anomaly in our laws is, that under the present

quota restriction there is no limitation upon the number of immigrants who may come here from countries in the Western Hemisphere. Some of our employers have found this loophole and are now experimenting with labor of low mental attainments, brought in numbers from a contiguous country. It is true that these men are willing to work for low wages, but employers who have had experience with them assure me that one workman of the American standard can do two and one-half times as much real work in a day as one of those natives of a semi-tropical land. There is little payroll economy in that sort of labor.

Part of our present immigration problem arises largely through the so-called "bootlegging" of aliens. I have before me estimates which place the number of aliens who surreptitiously enter the United States at one hundred daily. Some estimates run as high as one thousand a day which would exceed the number permissible under the quota law.

A study of the army intelligence tests applied to foreign-born soldiers during the war would indicate that in the last thirty-three years, America has accepted nearly fourteen million aliens of all types in order to acquire 7,572,857 who are of the type of low average intelligence or above. In other words, each year during that period we have received about 229,480 aliens of the higher grades of intelligence, or nearly as many as the number annually admitted under the 3 per cent quota law.

Our records of outgoing aliens date only from 1908, but by taking the figures since 1908 and certain steamship passenger records on file for a time previous to that, it is estimated that thirty went our for every hundred that came in during the years from 1890 to February 28, 1923. This puts the total number of emigrants at 6,450,656 and the number of immigrants who remained in the United States at 13,329,339.

Now, to protect the United States from bad immigration and to assure, so far as possible, that we shall get good immigration, I propose that we establish strict, but just tests of physical and mental health, and that we take those tests under the numerical restriction now placed by law on immigration. I would have those tests made abroad in order that the applicant for admission may not have to spend the earnings of a lifetime on a long sea voyage, in order to find out whether or not he can enter the United States. The solicitor of the department is inquiring into the possibility of moving our whole examining machinery to foreign countries under our present law. I feel that nothing would strengthen our whole immigration policy so much as this move. One great result of moving our inspection machinery abroad to make selections among the applicants for admission to America would be to end the heartrending scenes which every day confront our agents at Ellis Island and other ports of entry. Law enforcement is made particularly difficult when officials are faced with the sufferings and sorrows of the unfortunates who have traveled thousands of miles, leaving behind all that life has meant to them up to that time, only to find that under the law they are barred from the Promised Land. Rejection for many of them means utter poverty, a long return sea voyage, and despair. But the law is inexorable. And we could end all these horrors if we could make our selection on the other side. If we halt these cases before they leave their native countries we shall end the troubles at our ports of entry and the immigrant will be qualified to land in the United States immediately upon his arrival. I call this selective immigration. As long as the United States is to admit foreigners, I would have our system function to bring us the best class we can obtain abroad, and to make their way in America easy and comfortable.

I would also provide for enrollment of the alien after he is here. I would have him enrolled upon his admission, and, over a period of years, provide for a census of the alien population by the Naturalization Bureau. We register every American citizen to ascertain his right to exercise the suffrage and we provide for the compulsory education of our youth. Surely there can be no objection to the enrollment of an alien who comes with a desire to qualify for American citizenship. If, after a period of years, the record of the individual plainly showed that he was unfit, I would provide for his deportion.

I am not in favor of compelling any individual to become a citizen of the United States. Merely forcing an alien to go through the formal legal ceremony of naturalization will not make him an American. True citizenship must come from the mind and heart.

USES OF LABOR SHORTAGE[1]

The demands upon American production, both for home consumption and for exportation, have increased rapidly since 1914. It would be possible to show that the rate of increase has been greater than in the period preceding the war, in spite of the deficit in the import of labor. We do not, however, maintain the thesis that production has got on better without those two and a half million alien laborers than it would have got on with them. America might have made still more remarkable strides in production if nothing had happened to reduce the influx of alien labor. The cardinal point here is that America is capable of vigorous growth without the artificial stimulus of imported labor.

So much for results. But one is puzzled as to how it was done. There cannot have been so large a proportion of our workers unemployed, or partially employed, in 1920-1922 as in 1910-1914. Probably the high price of labor stimulated managers to find more ra-

[1] From the New Republic. February 14, 1923. p. 310-1.

tional ways of handling it. Probably an impetus has been given to the application of labor saving machinery. The efficiency engineers long ago demonstrated that the waste of potential labor power in industry is scandalous. Blocking the easy road of labor importation concentrates the attention of management upon the problems of economy of labor. That is all to the good. Still more to the good is the reduction in unemployment.

But what is much more important is the effect upon the general social-economic position of the working class. The alien labor of pre-war times was an instrument of production, indeed, but it was also a weapon in the hands of the employer to beat down the demands of American and Americanized labor. The practices of the coal and steel barons are too notorious to need more than mention. The twelve-hour day and starvation wages are direct corollaries of the unrestrained immigration of the period before 1914. If we can hold the gates closed for another decade, those abuses are bound to go.

Not everybody in America would like this. Nor would everybody in America be pleased with another natural consequence of restriction, that it will draw more and more negroes out of the rural south, especially the lynching belt, for common labor in the industries. Still another consequence is the strengthening of the trade unions. What happens when the whole working body in an industry is American or thoroughly Americanized is exemplified in the four great railway Brotherhoods. The "master and man" relation no longer obtains in the railway industry, but instead the relation of man and man. If there is anywhere in the world a body of men more self-respecting and more capable of commanding respect for their rights than the Brotherhood membership, we regret that it has escaped our notice.

If the immigration dikes hold, we shall presently have more trades as firmly organized, as dangerous to trifle with, as alive to their personal rights and public duties as the railway men. That may not be best for production. Mr. Gary might not get out as much steel and as large steel profits if he had to do business with men like Chief Stone.

But the real need of America is something other than abundance of steel and coal, woolens and cottons, gewgaws and gimcracks. America needs men, men who can stand as upright under physical labor as under any other respectable form of effort. And we shall get them by the Brotherhood plan, not by the Gary plan. But while we are holding up the alien tide to enable the American workman to establish himself in a position of self-respect comporting with the ideals of democracy, we need not despair of abundant production. It was long ago demonstrated, even to the satisfaction of the slave owners, that the slave cannot match the hired laborer in productiveness. It will yet be demonstrated that the most productive of men is the man who is really free.

SHALL WE LET DOWN THE BARS [1]

The question arises as to whether the best interests of American industry will be served by again letting down the bars to the unskilled, uneducated hordes of southeastern Europe. Is the solution of this problem not more likely to be found in the greater use, and broader application of labor-saving machinery?

What is to be said for this suggested solution? Let us first stress the fact that labor-saving machinery is primarily a substitute for common, unskilled labor. Machines are seldom used to replace skilled workers, but are used to increase their output. On the other hand, a single mechanical unit in the hands of a skilled worker will do the work of many unskilled hands. Thus the increased utilization of machinery would have the doubly beneficial effect of decreasing the demand of unskilled labor, and increasing the skilled labor requirement.

[1] By C. Coapes Brinley, Sales Engineer, Gifford-Wood Co., New York. From article in Industrial Management. April, 1923. p. 247-9.

Machinery, and particularly labor-saving machinery, is peculiarly an American product. We have led in mechanical development, but have we led in the application of our own developments? There are those who claim that, industrially, Germany has profited more by our mechanical genius than have we. However that may be, the fact is evident that America has hardly begun to substitute machinery for common labor. Compare, for example, the proportion of unskilled labor in the Ford motor plants with that in the average American industrial plant. Detailed figures are not available, but in the rough the comparison is a staggering revelation of general industrial inefficiency. The thing that the Ford group have accomplished is not inapplicable to practically the whole of American industry. The first step in this direction is to change the attitude of the manufacturer toward machinery; to overcome the inertia of custom. Strange as it may seem, there are several manufacturers of labor-saving devices who have failed to make the fullest application of their own product to their own plant.

An illustration of the American manufacturer's attitude toward labor-saving machinery may be had from the experience of a machinery salesman who interviewed the manager of a branch factory for one of the largest corporations in the country. The subject under consideration was the handling of coal from cars on the railroad siding to the boiler house bin. After obtaining the current cost of handling the coal by hand, the salesman presented indisputable figures which showed, after due allowances for interest on the investment, insurance, depreciation, etc., a net saving of 20 per cent. The Manager's reply was that he could not recommend an investment unless he could show his company a net return of 40 per cent! This is of course an extreme instance, and happened in early 1920, when business was booming, and unskilled labor rather plentiful. Nevertheless it is largely typical of the American business mind on this subject.

Another point to be stressed is that machinery being so almost entirely an American product, a considerable application of labor-saving devices would greatly develop a purely domestic industry, and aid the general business revival. The money invested in American machinery would go into American homes, from there into American shops and so back into American industry. On the other hand a considerable portion of the money paid to imported unskilled labor is sent abroad to relatives, for which we get no material return, and which serves only to turn the foreign exchange rate against us.

Finally, the important thing to be stressed is the fact that the substitution of machinery for unskilled labor, of course only as far as practicable, is a permanent solution of the problem now confronting the American manufacturer. Machinery "stays put." It does not go out on strike, it cannot decide to go to Europe, or take a job in the next town. It does, however, deteriorate, and accumulate carrying charges when not in use; so also, it might be said, does labor. The difference here is that the manufacturer stands these charges on machinery, and labor carries itself through the periods of unemployment and after its span of usefulness. But the trend of social legislation in this country today is toward taking this burden from the shoulders of labor and placing it directly, or indirectly through Federal aid, on the shoulders of industry. Thus American industry has to decide ultimately whether it wants to carry machinery, or imported common labor, over the recurring periods of depression.

THE NEGRO LABOR AND THE IMMIGRANT[1]

From all available, accurate data the negro achieved a new position in the calculations of industrial managers, north and south, during the war. Eighty-seven out of

[1] In the Survey. May 14, 1921. p. 209-10.

every one hundred negroes ten years of age and over were wage earners in 1910. The negro speaks English. He is 100 per cent American in feeling and ideas as shown by his sacrifices in every war from that on Boston Common where the negro, Crispus Attucks, fell, down to the fields of France where thousands paid the supreme price of loyalty to the flag. No "Americanization" is needed for him except to see that he is accorded the opportunities, rights and privileges of an American citizen.

Some facts recently published by the Department of Labor in a study, The Negro at Work During the World War and During Reconstruction, give firm ground for the view that on the whole the negro has made good during the war in many of the basic industries such as iron and steel, ship-building, slaughtering and meat packing. The negro worker shared very largely in war production. More than twenty-four thousand negro men were employed in the shipyards under the supervision of the Emergency Fleet Corporation. The packing houses of Chicago increased the percentage of their negro labor from two- to five-fold during the three years preceding 1919 and at last accounts the percentage of negroes among their total employees was near the higher levels.

The recorded opinion of the large majority of thirty-eight superintendents and managers of large industrial plants were that negro workers showed ambition for advancement when encouraged by the opportunity; that in work where materials were handled there was little or no difference in the loss of materials due to defective workmanship; that, as a rule, it took about the same amount of time for breaking in new white workers as for new negro workers. The concensus of opinion of these employers of more than one hundred thousand white workers and more than seven thousand negro workers, mainly in unskilled and semi-skilled work, after their experience with both races was that, all things considered, negro workers had been nearly as satisfactory as white workers on the same jobs and operations, and that in some cases the testimony showed that they had been more satisfactory.

The test of comparative average earnings per week and of comparative average number of hours worked per week in twenty-three plants in six basic industries showed that negro workers not only held their own but in some operations surpassed white workers in the same plants. During war times negro unskilled workers were largely employed in war industries in twelve southern states and fourteen northern states. Only twenty-three firms out of a total of two hundred and ninety-two of these firms that employed negroes reported less than 50 per cent war work.

It is true that the negro is not yet accustomed to the rigid routine of the modern industrial plant. He still suffers from the slipshod habits and uncertain ways of the slave plantation, the tenant farm and the small-town activities. The encouraging thing, however, is the rapidity with which he learns new customs and methods of work and the happy, easy way he has of adapting himself quickly to new conditions.

The preceding facts relate to negro men. Negro women workers have made quite as good a record. Visits made by special agents of the Women's Bureau of the Department of Labor, to selected establishments in 1918-1919 and in 1920 show this to be true. In 1919 visits were made in one hundred and fifty-two establishments employing 21,547 negro women. The largest numbers were employed in tobacco plants, textile and clothing factories, laundries, hardware and glassware establishments and in office work.

In 1920 about two years after the Armistice, a second round of visits was made to one hundred and fifty selected plants employing more than eleven thousand negro women. These were engaged mainly in the same types of industry as those visited nearly two years before, although the same plants were not always included and others were substituted. The large number of negro women still employed during the present slump indicates that they have given sufficient satisfaction to keep a foothold in industry even when unemployment is widespread.

The significance of the place the negro woman has secured in industry in relation to immigration and the future of the race in industrial labor may be illustrated by the clothing trade in New York where so many foreign-born women are employed. Ten years ago a careful survey made by the writer in that city revealed hardly a negro woman in such factories except occasionally on other than trade operations. Today, literally hundreds, if not thousands, are employed and in many factories without restrictions on the operations they may perform.

SELECTING CITIZENS[1]

If the boys and girls who are educated in our schools refuse to have anything to do with labour, what chance is there that the children of the millions we are urged to bring to our shores in the next ten years will learn any different lesson? If their offspring in turn insist upon joining the ranks of the white-collared, we shall have to multiply the millions to be imported from other lands to do the heavy labour for their children as well as for ours. Where would such a process end? The logical conclusion is that when our land is so full of individuals, educated in American schools, that there will be no place to wedge in ignorant foreigners to do the work for them, our civilization will inevitably collapse. We should all have become such perfect ladies

[1] By Cornelia James Cannon. North American Review. September, 1923. p. 325-33.

and gentlemen by that time that we would inevitably freeze and starve for lack of the humble of other lands to warm and feed us. The assumption in the minds of these pseudo-economists is that the American's distaste for manual labour is stronger than his instinct for self preservation.

Why must we postpone the eventual day of reckoning? Why not assume that the problem must be solved with the population we have today, with no prospect of additions save such as come from home production? There seems no reason why we should not be a "self-contained" nation as are other nations. We have too long allowed ourselves to be stampeded by the American industrialist, and have risked the lowering of our ultimate quality as a nation by making concessions to keep our factories running day and night.

In the first place, whence comes the theory that second generation Americans have an inherent aversion to manual labour? Those of us who go camping in the summer or who live in simple country homes find ourselves able and willing to do with equanimity all the skilled and unskilled work that ordinary living requires. Many of us, who have been educated in the public schools and are thus assumed to have developed abhorrence for such activities, begin, during the summer vacation, to suspect that our *métier* is garbage and ash collection, waste disposal and hoeing, with carpentering, painting, plumbing, and occasional plastering and bricklaying thrown in as side lines.

If, in the second place, the shortage in these fields of human achievement continues, as it bids fair to do, until the pay of the plasterer approximates that of the bank president, the skilled trades will return to the position of dignified social recognition they received before the influx of ignorant and helpful foreigners. The fact that in the recent past such work has been relegated to the classes accorded neither full social nor civic fellowship has brought the work itself into a category of disrepute which made the children of the workers in turn unwilling to engage in it. It was not that the work itself was necessarily unattractive; nor that it failed to present itself to the eye of imagination as a worthy form of service and means of livelihood; the difficulty has been due to the fact that certain types of labour have been regarded as the special province of the foreign-born upon whom the philistine American looks down. As a result manual labour has asquired a fictitious inferiority in the minds of the ordinary unthinking person. To continue the very conditions which have produced the revolt against hand labour by opening wide the gates to the immigrant only postpones the day of real adjustment, and enormously multiplies the difficulties.

The pressure for fresh supplies of foreign labour recurringly insists that we have nowhere near so large a population as our territory can support, that we must be constantly growing if we wish to prosper, and that there are waste places to be filled, deserts to be watered, and hills to be cut down before we can call ours a finished country. The simple lover of his native land may wonder what is the hurry, may even acclaim the glory of the imperfect, but he is brushed aside by the enthusiast for efficiency. One fundamental seems to be lost sight of by these special pleaders. They ignore the part the waste places of this country play in the spiritual life of the nation. The mountains, the deserts, the unbroken prairie, are an asset to every man, woman, and child in the United States, a treasure whose value cannot be reckoned in dollars but is evidenced in the whole spirit and outlook of our people. We are under no compulsion to populate and utilize these unappropriated lands. Their very presence endows us with optimism, with faith in ourselves, with an enlarging sense of opportunity. They protect our young men from the shutting down of life, the narrowing horizon which accompanies density of population. The consciousness of ample physical background enables us to preserve an ardency of hope and confidence, that at its worst is no more than over-enthusiasm, and at its best is the power that can reinspire a weary world.

The filling up and harnessing to production of the rest of this country would represent a gain in taxable property undoubtedly, but it would mean irreparable loss through a closing in of the possibilities of life to our whole nation. Our waste places are the source of much of the radiance and youth, of the optimism and generosity of our people. Once they are lost to us, age and the inward look will be upon us.

We have questions to ask of the biologists, which they must some day answer for us. Can we, with a very diverse human stock which has no stable uniform base, construct a society with a homogeneous spiritual and moral quality? Western civilization grafted upon the Japanese has produced unlovely fruit. The Occidental mind may have developed antitoxins, natural to its growth, which save it from being thus poisoned by its own civilization. Do the different races of the Occident have likewise each a capacity to absorb without harm the ideals which they have generated themselves, accompanied by an inability to absorb their neighbours' ideals without disaster? It is an historical enigma whether Mohammedanism spread only among those radically fitted to accept it; whether the European could have been appealed to by the teachings of Mohammed; and whether, if the Europeans had become Mohammedans, the religion itself would have been profoundly modified, or the people accepting it.

Similarly we must consider, not as idle speculation but as a matter of vital concern to our future, whether our civilization, with its distinctively Anglo-Saxon foundation, depends upon the presence in our midst of those racially akin to the founders, or whether the form of any society is independent of the mental, physical or spiritual inheritance of its members.

We have made a tentative answer to this question by excluding the Asiatic from entry into this country and from citizenship even if he is here. This exclusion takes no count of the superiority or inferiority of the races involved. It does perhaps pay tribute to the intolerance of the inhabitants of the excluding country. We are confessedly unable to live happily and without dangerous friction with races so different from ourselves as the natives of Asia. The common sense decision is to eliminate so far as possible the causes of conflict. There is no ethical principle involved in the exclusion of the Asiatic; the matter is purely one of expediency. The ethical principle is called into play when the question comes of the treatment of the Asiatics or the individuals of any other race once they are admitted to the country. There expediency must subordinate itself to a higher imperative.

The exclusion from this country of any other race falls in the same category as the exclusion of the Asiatic. If the admission of any racial group complicates our problems or jeopardizes the success of the experiment in organizing a democratic society we are endeavouring to work out, we are perfectly justified, indeed obligated, to practice exclusion.

Some sentimentalists urge the wide open door on the basis of offering refuge to the down-trodden and suffering of the earth, and of relieving the congestion of Europe. We have however a responsibility to our children and to those who are already here superior to the claims of any other human beings. The possible menace potential citizens might be to us must carry more weight in our decisions than the suffering of those same individuals as the result of conditions over which we have no control, and for which we are not responsible. Any hope of relieving the congestion of Europe by taking the year's surplus is a never ending task. We have never had any effect in reducing European congestion: the population of countries which have sent us large numbers of immigrants has simply increased to make up the loss.

GREAT FALLACY OF IMMIGRATION[1]

The idea too widely prevails that the United States has been made by immigration, that without the millions pouring in from Europe the nation could never have reached its present greatness, that our agriculture and our industries could not have been developed, and that our population would still be limited to a thin strip along the Atlantic seacoast. This, however, has not been the experience of other countries which for a hundred years have admitted practically no immigrants. Take England, for example. At the beginning of the 19th century its population was eight million; in a hundred years this had grown to thirty-two million. This growth was not the result of immigration; it represented the natural increase of the native population, automatically responding to increased economic resources and consequently increased food supply. Far from adding to its population from immigration England, during this same period, sent millions of its peoples to other lands, especially the United States, Canada, and Australia. In Germany, the experience has been the same. The population of the German Empire in 1870 was forty-two million; by 1914—forty-four years—this had grown to sixty-eight million. Immigration had little to do with this growth; as in the case of England, Germany all this time was losing large numbers of her population to the United States. The early history of the United States emphasizes the same point. We started with

[1] From World's Work. June, 1923. p. 121-2.

four million in 1790; by 1850 this had grown to twenty-three million; in that sixty years only about two million immigrants had come to this country, and three-fourths —or one and one-half million—had arrived between 1840 and 1850. These figures therefore indicate that the native American population had increased from four million to at least twenty million in fifty years—or about five-fold. Thus it is apparent that the original population, in accordance with the forecasts of Washington and his contemporaries, was increasing in sufficient ratio to keep pace with the growth in our economic and agricultural resources.

The point can therefore be maintained that, had there been no immigration at all, the United States might be just as populous as it is at present, the only difference being that our one hundred and ten million people would all be the descendants of the four million with which we started our national life.

HOW IMMIGRATION AFFECTS BUSINESS[1]

The American Federation of Labor has declared that the talk of a labor shortage is propaganda intended to bring about a reduction of wages. Oliver Hoyem says in the American Federationist:

> The truth of the matter is that the steel industry wants the cheapest labor of Europe and prefers the inferior mental types because experience has proved that most of them do not possess sufficient intelligence to organize for their own protection. The instinct of organization, so highly developed among the workmen of Sweden, Germany, England and France, has not been developed among the people of southeastern Europe. They can be treated like sheep and herded around the gates at a steel plant as a perpetual menace to the rise of every organization of union labor.
>
> Tide after tide of cheap, oppressed, foreign labor has swept over the steel industry of Pennsylvania. Each succeeding tide of cheap labor has been characterized by a lower level of intelligence. Scotch, Irish and Cornish labor replaced the original

[1] From Industrial Digest. February, 1923. p. 96-7.

American labor and these in turn have been driven out by other cheap labor, until now the immigration which is urged to enter the steel industry contains a large percentage of the most backward peoples of Europe and Asia. Logically the next tide should consist of Asiatics, and undoubtedly it would long ago have been composed of Chinese, and Hindoo labor, except that the laws of the country constituted a bar. If permissible many employers would bring in coolie labor just as the sugar planters of Hawaii are clamoring for more Chinese coolie labor.

Henry Ford also thinks that the campaign to change the immigration laws is the evil propaganda of Big Business. His Dearborn Independent says:

Certain sections of Big Business are beginning a campaign for the abandonment of immigration restrictions, alleging a threatened shortage of common labor. The inconsistency of this with high tariff legislation to keep out the product of European labor is so apparent that a mere allusion should be sufficient. It is the paradox of economics that Big Business claims to champion the American wage-earner by excluding the product of foreign factories, while bringing into direct competition here the foreign labor itself. It is equally paradoxical to expect to maintain an American wage level, with the foreign market closed or partially closed in retaliation.

But the plan is neither paradoxical nor inconsistent, when the motive is realized. Big Business seeks cheap labor, not only to gain larger profits, but to hold the threat of unemployment over American workmen. Nothing so subdues a worker as an army of job-hunters hungry for his place. So, the emergency Congress is to be called upon to open wide the gates, not to actual immigrants desirous to make homes and become citizens, but to hordes of every class who cross the ocean only to gather together what seems to them a fortune, with which some day to return to the homeland and a life of ease they could never wrest from home employment.

They will endure privations here for a time to amass the means of enjoying the future. Many will be disappointed, for the lure is a false one; many will become, if not already, recruits to the ranks of the lawless; many will return despondent; while our own labor will be degraded. But if Big Business wins, the transatlantic liners will be crowded and unscrupulous immigration agents will reap a large harvest.

Why Immigration Should Be Restricted

Professor Henry R. Seager of Columbia University, also a restrictionist, presented his opinion clearly and fairly at a joint discussion meeting of the American Economic Association and the Management Division of the American Society of Mechanical Engineers:

The arguments for letting down the bars and allowing the hundreds of thousands of laborers we could undoubtedly employ to enter are, from a business point of view, very strong. By maintaining or even advancing our standards of admission as regards physical fitness we could undoubtedly secure in large numbers just the type of sturdy and docile workers for which our industries are now clamoring. Accustomed to much lower wages than prevail in this country, these men would accept with enthusiasm current rates of pay, and the trend of wages upward which is proving embarrassing to our reviving iron and steel, copper mining, and other industries would be checked. Moreover, immigrant labor, from a national point of view, is always cheap labor. Other countries have borne the cost of rearing immigrants during the unproductive years of childhood, and in admitting them in early manhood we reap the full benefit of this investment without having to contribute anything to it.

There can be no question, then, that a return to our more liberal pre-war immigration policy would enable us to increase substantially our output of goods, and of this large output a goodly share over the wages we should have to pay for immigrant labor would remain as profits to employers and investors and constitute a net addition to our national wealth.

Notwithstanding these certain material advantages, economists very generally oppose a return to our former liberal immigration law and for reasons with which we are all familiar.

In this matter there is much more at stake than our national wealth. It goes to the very heart of our national welfare. Although most of us did not realize it, the admission of an average of a million immigrants a year before the war came dangerously near to wrecking our country, politically, socially, and economically. In saying this I do not intend to assert that our native Americans are demonstrably superior to the immigrants who come to our shores even from southeastern Europe. What is certain is that they are more familiar with our institutions, more generally convinced that these should be maintained, and better trained in their operation.

Clearly we need a respite from adding further to the number of our population of the routine manual laboring type and should concentrate all the time and attention we can spare upon means by which we can prevent the 45,000,000 at the bottom of the intelligence scale from further multiplying while we increase the thirteen and a half million of superior intelligence until they become the predominant American type. Unless we thus deliberately subordinate our goods or wealth interests to our national-welfare interests the rights to life, liberty, and the pursuit of happiness, which we still consider our most precious national inheritance, will lose their only certain sanction, a representative government responsive to an intelligent as well as independent citizenship.

IMMIGRATION—OR MACHINERY [1]

In seeking for the solution of his own private problems, the individual manufacturer can get valuable enlightenment from the recently published report on the immigration problem based on an investigation conducted by the National Industrial Conference Board of New York. The economists, statisticians and sociologists of this board, acting under the direction of Magnus W. Alexander, have conducted a disinterested and painstaking research of the whole immigration problem of the United States since records were made. They have reported without bias the facts as they have found them, and have not diminished the value of their work by recommending any legislative or other panaceas to give immediate and sure relief.

The first vital fact that we get from the Industrial Conference Board is that the birth rate in the United States is not sufficiently high to produce workers fast enough to supply the growing demand of American industries. As there is small likelihood that the birth rate will increase, but two alternatives present themselves. Either we must open our doors to workers from other lands, in other words, stimulate immigration, or we must find some means of increasing the individual output of every available worker here.

Assuming for the moment that the manufacturer must depend upon immigration for his additional labor supply, let us see where we stand as regards the immediate present. The law under which immigrants are at present entering the United States limits the number coming from a given country in any calendar year to 3 per cent of the foreign-born members of that race living in the United States at the time of the 1910 census.

[1] By K. H. Condit, editor, American Machinist. American Machinist. March 15, 1923. p. 393-5.

Another provision of the law limits the number entering in any one month to 20 per cent of the quota for the year. The supporters of the 3 per cent limit law had in mind not only the general limitation of immigration, but the reduction of the percentage of southern European immigrants and the increase of the percentage of immigrants from northwestern Europe in the number let in in any given period.

The effect of the new law in limiting the total number of immigrants is illustrated by the fact that during the fiscal year of 1920, 805,228 immigrants arrived, while 247,718 emigrants departed, leaving a net increase of population by immigration of 557,510. During the first fiscal year of the law's operation, the year ending June 30, 1922, 309,556 immigrants came in while 198,712 emigrants left, making a net increase of population by immigration of only 110,844. It will be seen that the gain was less than one-fifth that of the preceding year.

Net Loss in Common Labor

But this is by no means the whole story. Analysis of the immigrants and emigrants by profession or occupation shows that under the 3 per cent law, there has been a net gain in professional and skilled labor classes and a large net loss in the common labor class. In other words, instead of gaining common laborers through immigration, we are actually losing more than we gain because of the return of men of this class, mostly Italians and Poles, to their native countries.

Various attempts have been made to soften the restrictions of the 3 per cent law by amendment, but without success. Organized labor is, of course, strongly in favor of drastic restrictions for more or less selfish reasons. But, in addition, there are many disinterested citizens who believe that the sociological problems connected with the arrival of many thousands of unassimilable immigrants are far more dangerous to the country as a whole than the economic hardship caused by an insufficient labor supply. It is almost inconceivable that any change in the 3 per cent law can take effect before the end of the next fiscal year, which ends June 30, 1924, as the last Congress expired March 4, without taking action, and the President is strongly against calling a special session.

For the present, then, the manufacturer has no recourse but to turn to the other alternative already mentioned, the increasing of the individual output of the men available. This factor also divides itself into two parts, better management and better equipment. Much can probably be done by improving methods of management. In the series of articles, "What's Wrong With the Railroad Shops?" it was brought out that in very few cases were either men or machines producing anywhere near their capacity, and what was said of railroad shops in this respect applies with equal force to many other shops.

More and Better Machinery Necessary

While better management may do much to help ease the present situation, it cannot go the whole way and more and better machinery must be relied upon to do the rest. There are in this country many ingenious machines that do the work of many men, but their number must be multiplied if our industries are not to suffer. We must apply the kind of brains that produce the big lake ore carriers, which load and unload themselves by means of elevators and conveyors in periods of a few hours, to some of our other problems. It is said that the crops of 1922 were the largest ever produced in the United States, and that the relative number of men engaged in harvesting them was the smallest on record. Apparently, the farmer is learning by dire necessity the value of agricultural machinery for doing the heavy work of the farm. Some of our manufacturers might profit from a study of the way the farmer has replaced unskilled labor with machinery.

Let's forget our present problems for the moment and take a look at the future. The extension of the 3 per cent limit act expires June 30, 1924, and consequently, a new immigration law must be passed before that time. Judging from the immigration legislation which the House Immigration Committee attempted to have the expiring Congress pass, our policy of restricting the number of aliens coming to our shores is not likely to suffer any radical change.

There are good reasons for believing that immigration restriction will be a permanent policy. The objection of the American Federation of Labor is sure to continue, because it is founded on the very real fear of its members that the competition of cheap alien labor will reduce the standard of living of the American working man. That this fear is a reasonable one is shown by a recent survey of housing conditions where it was found that the average rental paid by the immigrant family was appreciably less than that paid by the American working man with a family, and that the immigrants were content to squeeze more people into a room than were the Americans. Another factor that should be taken into consideration is the effect of the ignorance of the immigrant of the language and customs in his new home, on labor conditions in the factories and plants where he works. Unscrupulous foremen exact tribute from him for increases in pay, better jobs and retention in times of unemployment. The bad effect of this practice on the plant morale is obvious.

The Feeling Against Immigration

The membership of the American Federation of Labor, however, is entirely too small to account for the force that lies behind the immigration restriction idea. Always excepting the employers who need a steady flow of cheap labor to operate their plants and expand them to keep up with the industrial growth of the nation, there is an almost universal feeling against unlimited immigration. This feeling may readily be explained by the fact that a great majority of the people already here belong to a different race from that to which the majority of our immigrants, under the unlimited restriction prior to the enactment of the present law, belong. The new boy on the block is always looked upon with suspicion by the old gang.

There is also a pretty general feeling that the proportion of illiteracy, insanity, pauperism and crime is greater among the recent arrivals than among the native. As a matter of fact, statistics show this criticism to be unjust. The balance swings the other way. The percentage of illiteracy, it is true, was much greater until the present law went into effect, but the percentages of insanity and pauperism are lower and the list of crimes committed include far more of the less serious offences which are probably due to ignorance of the law rather than intent.

Another criticism aimed against the immigrant is that he sends most of his earnings back home. It is quite natural that he should, and it is certainly not an unmitigated evil for certain European countries to find in the money sent back by their emigrant sons the only means of balancing their budgets.

On the other hand, there are some things to be said in favor of the immigrant. His principal object in coming here is to work. Rather more than half of the recent immigrants are males between the ages of sixteen and sixty-four. The great number who come here without families are not tied to any one part of the country and consequently add to the fluidity of the labor supply. They, therefore, aid to a certain extent in solving the unemployment problem, because when jobs become scarce in one locality, they can easily move to another where a different situation exists.

There is a sentiment in some quarters to change the

basis upon which the 3 per cent limit is calculated from gross to net immigration. That this would have a profound effect upon the character of our immigration is clear from the emigration figures, which, as already mentioned, show a great number of the common labor class going home each year.

Such a change would undoubtedly add to the supply of common labor, but it would also tend to develop a peon class of migratory labor most undesirable from the social and political point of view. Such labor would flow to this country when work was plentiful, and flow back during hard times. It would come here with no intention of remaining or of adapting itself to our methods and adding to our national wealth. It would live in labor camps and would be practically untouched by any of our various Americanization and betterment projects. Worst of all, it would probably be exploited to an extent hitherto undreamed of, and the consequences might be extremely dangerous.

Another plan, and a promising one, would retain the present 3 per cent limitation but would permit an additional 2 per cent chosen on a selective basis to come in. One of the bases of selection would be a demonstrated need for immigrants of a particular kind. They might be farm laborers, or men for railway maintenance or for steel mills, and they would have to meet physical, mental and moral tests. This plan would add a certain amount of flexibility to the present one and would afford a test of the possibilities of selection.

An ideal immigration law so drawn as to carry out an enlightened immigration policy, when we develop one, would supply sufficient high-grade workers for the needs of industry and at the same time would not add to our sociological and political problems. Selective examination before the prospective immigrant was permitted to board ship for the United States would be an intrinsic part of such a policy.

American institutions rest solely on good citizenship. They were created by people who had a background of self-government. New arrivals should be limited to our capacity to absorb them into the ranks of good citizenship. America must be kept American. For this purpose it is necessary to continue a policy of restricted immigration. It would be well to make such immigration of a selective nature with some inspection at the source, and based either on a prior census or upon the record of naturalization. Either method would insure the admission of those with the largest capacity and best intention of becoming citizens. I am convinced that our present economic and social conditions warrant a limitation of those to be admitted. We should find additional safety in a law requiring the immediate registration of all aliens. Those who do not want to be partakers of the American spirit ought not to settle in America.—*From President Coolidge's message to Congress, delivered December* 6, 1923.

WILL RESTRICTIVE IMMIGRATION THROTTLE INDUSTRY?[1]

The recurring industrial depressions of the business cycle are usually ushered in by two phenomena: one is overproduction as compared with current demand, and the other is the advance of prices to an unbearable degree. These two factors usually run together, but sometimes one leads or is more influential than the other.

As things are going now, the first general check to the new era of prosperity that is upon us will come from increasing prices rather than from overproduction. Generally speaking, I believe that all authorities are agreed that, after two or three years of starvation consumption in this country, there is very little danger of

[1] By R. C. Marshall, Jr. General Manager, Associated General Contractors of America. Constructor. November, 1922. p. 12-13.

our getting to a point where normal stocks will be restored and normal consumption resumed within two or three years at least.

Generally it may be said that it is extreme and feverish commercial and industrial activity which results in a surplus of goods that dams up the current of the industrial stream and causes a rapid increase in labor and other production costs; but now the situation seems to be the reverse. Although it was only a year ago that President Harding felt it his duty to call a national conference to consider what to do about the industrial unemployment situation that then existed we have today—before anything like an industrial boom has appeared—a practical shortage of labor. This labor shortage is very marked in the building trades (as is evidenced by many instances of contractors bidding against one another for workmen) and has become so acute in the iron and steel industry that many steel companies have recently announced voluntary wage increases, caused by the necessity of holding their men against the inducements held out by other employers.

No Parallel in History

I do not believe that there is a parallel to this situation in the whole of our national history. With business failures still running 50 per cent above normal, with unfilled steel tonnage 19 per cent below normal, with the whole agricultural population still suffering severely from deflation of the prices of its products, and with many other evidences that we are not yet back on an even plane of prosperity, we find ourselves confronted by a labor shortage and rising labor costs. Already, in from three to six months, increasing labor and material prices have very noticeably increased building costs long before they had lowered to what we thought was a reasonable basis; and the danger symptoms of bonus payments to workmen and of competitive bidding for labor by industrial groups again appear. As wages are approximately 44 per cent of the direct cost of building, the effect of their increase on construction costs is at once evident.

In cities such as New York and Chicago, contractors are paying from $2 to $3 a day in excess of the agreed scale of wages to secure sufficient common labor. As a result, common labor is receiving $8 and $9 for an eight-hour day. As a result, skilled workers are becoming restive and any effort to bring construction wages into line with decreasing costs in other industries is stubbornly resisted.

Why?

Why, it may be asked, should the nation, after two years of business quiescence, so suddenly jump from a plethora of labor to an embarrassing shortage?

A complete answer to this question would deal with many factors, such as the restriction of immigration, the shifting of population back from industrial centers to the farm, the decreased productiveness of American labor, the extraordinary vigor of the demand for goods consequent upon the unusually complete exhaustion of stocks during depression, and the reassertion of shortage caused by the war and not yet filled, although suppressed during the past two years.

Restriction of Immigration

Of these factors, especially when considered with a view to the future, restriction of immigration is by all odds the most important. An examination of the immigration figures as reported by the Department of Labor reveals the astounding fact that for the twelve months ending with last June the net immigration was only 88,250, and that there was an actual loss of about ten thousand in men, the surplus of immigration over emigration being only in women and children. It is true that the present immigration restriction law, which limits the number of persons who may come into this country from across the seas to 3 per cent of the total number of aliens of those regions living in the United States in 1910, does contemplate the annual entry of three hundred and sixty thousand persons. In fact, the actual admissions from Old World countries fall considerably below the number permitted by the law because those who wish to come here from many of those countries are fewer than their allotted quota, while the would-be immigrants from other countries are more numerous than their quotas. The law does not permit the deficiency of the former class to be made up from the excess of the latter. The actual outcome, when emigration is deducted from immigration, is that the new law, instead of admitting 45 per cent of the normal population influx of other years, actually admits only 11 per cent; and, as I have already remarked, there is an actual net loss in men when emigration is taken into account. The effect, then, of the immigration law is not only to reduce the volume of incoming immigrant labor, but to wipe it out and in fact turn the current the other way. We are, then, actually undertaking a new era of industrial prosperity and activity with a diminishing instead of an increasing labor supply, so far as concerns our reliance upon foreign countries.

Alien Labor Continually Necessary

Even if our industrial activity in this country were not to expand, we need a certain volume of alien labor; and, if it is to go on growing as it has in the past, we must have a still larger volume of alien, and especially of common, laborers.

Labor is not a fixed caste in this country, and sons do not follow in their father's course in life. In Europe, where social class lines have long been crystalized, workmen's sons succeed their fathers and the labor supply is fairly steady and increases proportionately with the growing population of the nation as a whole. With us, on the contrary, the tendency is actually for the number of our native-born workmen to decrease as the population increases, because there is a continual shifting in this country from the callous-handed class to the white-collar class. Throughout our history, the main source of our common labor has been immigration. Skilled mechanics are not replaced from native sources as fast as they are eliminated by disability or death. The skilled American workman is not usually succeeded by his son. His place is often taken by the son of a foreign-born common laborer, so to restrict the supply of common labor is also to reduce the number of skilled workers.

In construction alone, we need approximately thirty-five thousand new skilled workers and also twelve thousand additional common laborers annually, merely to replace those lost by death or other causes. As construction employs about 22 per cent of the skilled and common laborers of all the mechanical and manufacturing industries, as classified by the United States Census Bureau, it is substantially the fact that this country requires not less than two hundred and fourteen thousand new manufacturing and mechanical workers annually to replace losses caused by death and retirement.

Annual Net Loss of Alien Adult Males

The population of this country is increasing at the rate of one million four hundred thousand annually, or about fourteen per thousand, so that to keep pace with the growth of population and its increasing requirements for goods and consequently for labor (without even considering higher standards of living which would increase consumption faster than population) the United States requires an addition of fourteen manual laborers annually per thousand already in the trade. Applying this rate to the eleven million men in manufacturing and the mechanical industries, we find that we must add one hundred and fifty-four thousand to the replacement figures above given, making a total of three hundred and sixty-eight thousand new workers needed annually.

Against this requirement we have at present a net increase due to immigration of only eighty-eight thousand five hundred and twenty women and children, and a net loss of adult males.

Then, again, of the men who enter the country under the present immigration law, the number of productive workers is negligible. Examination of the immigrants shows that only a small proportion of them are fit recruits for the manual labor of this country. This is due to the skill of certain racial groups, whose members belong to the trading and clerical class, in meeting the requirements of our present immigration laws, and to the fact that the immigrants must be able to read and write. Under educational conditions prevailing in large sections of Europe, this latter requirement ordinarily excludes the common laborer. The educational requirement was well intentioned, but it is not working out as intended. The actual net result is that it is admitting women and children and undersized feeble-bodied men of the clerical class, but very few real workers.

AMERICANS BY CHOICE[1]

Certain inferences and conclusions seem to be warranted on the whole by our examination and analyses of the compilations of the United States Census, the Immigration Commission of 1907, the Naturalization Bureau and the Americanization Study. It is not possible to reproduce here all the supporting tables.

First and most important is the destruction of the legendary presumption of some change for the worse in

[1] By John Palmer Gavit. Publication No. 227. 18p. pa. National Liberal Immigration League. New York. June, 1922.

recent years in the inherent character-quality of immigration to this country, and in the attitude of the typical immigrant of those years toward American citizenship. There has been no such change.

Second, it is evident that such difference as exists among races is not an inherent racial quality but a difference between the political, social and economic conditions at the time of migration in the country of origin. Those nations whose people are most free from tyranny and oppression and most contented with the conditions under which they live at home, send the fewest immigrants to America; their immigrants come at a later age, and when they do come they retain longest or altogether their original citizenship.

Third, and broadly corollary, is the fact that the major, not to say exclusively controlling, factor in the political absorption of the immigrant is *length of residence.* The longer the individual lives in America the more likely he is to seek active membership therein.

Fourth, the interval between arrival and petition for naturalization—or even the original declaration of intention—is much longer than has generally been supposed The average immigrant, regardless of racial extraction, does not concern himself about political privileges or activities until long years of residence and the attainment of a considerable degree of permanent social and economic status.

Fifth, whether from northwestern or from southeastern Europe, whether from the so-called "recent" or "older" immigration, the racial groups show a slower desire for citizenship and a lower rate of naturalization while they are employed in the more poorly-paid industries; both the individual interest and the rate increase as the individuals toil upward in the social and economic scale.

The inherent thing in the racial quality, experience and character of the immigrant that leads some to seek citizenship earlier than others; the essential element in the "quality of assimilability," in the display of "civic and political interest," is a human thing, which lies and always has lain broad upon the fact of nearly all of the statistical tables over which students have labored so intricately and pontificated so solemnly—in some instances so absurdly. It is a thing so obvious that it is difficult to understand why so many of them have overlooked it.

EFFICIENCY OF NEGRO AND MEXICAN LABORERS [1]

Because the immigration movement is now so restricted, a great part of the work of getting employees in the iron and steel industry has been associated with the migration movement of negroes and Mexicans from the south and southwest to the north. While this has been a source of some relief, iron and steel manufacturers have made known to the government officials their conviction that this class of labor will never acquire the efficiency of the typical steel mill laborer, such as the Slav. The statement has been made by an important iron and steel manufacturer that, rating the Slav at 100 per cent efficiency, the average colored worker in northern steel mills would be rated at 80 per cent while a considerably lower rating is given the Mexican laborer. Looked at from a point of loss of tonnage, it is maintained that the colored and Mexican laborers are extremely expensive, and especially at this particular time. when the iron and steel industry is fully engaged.

VIEWS OF THE MINORITY [2]

Ever since the 3 per cent restriction quota law and its amendments went into effect, just complaints from

[1] From "Keen Interest in the Coming of Immigrants," by L. W. Moffett. Iron Age. May 31, 1923. p. 1573.

[2] From 67th Congress. 4th Session. House. Report No. 1621. [To accompany S. 4092.]

every section of the country have been registered against its harsh, inhuman, and unworkable provisions. This was recognized by the Secretary of Labor and the Bureau of Immigration, who were compelled to urge the temporary admission of the wives and children of American citizens and declarants who had not been permitted to enter under the law, owing to its drastic provisions. Public opinion forced the adoption of two amendments which permitted the entry of several thousand Armenian refugees, yet a large number of refugees, as well as the wives and children of American citizens, were deported when the quota of 3 per cent had been reached. No consideration was given to the fact that many of them had left their homes long before they had any reason to believe or expect that the quota of the country of their nativity would be exhausted and although they had received their visés. The bill [S. 4092] in a measure aims to remedy the harsh provisions of the present law which caused so much suffering and to prevent in the future a repetition of the same unfortunate conditions. If this provision had been originally adopted, as some of us urged, much of the suffering of those held at Ellis Island and other ports of entry and finally deported would have been avoided. Consequently, we heartily approve the adoption of this provision, which will permit the near-blood relatives to enter as non-quota immigrants.

The provision allowing a basic quota of four hundred for all countries will prevent the return and deportation of peoples of small countries who especially have suffered under the unworkable provisions of the present law.

We also heartily approve of the provisions providing for the thorough examination and investigation of immigrants in the ports of embarkation before leaving for the United States, as well as the extremely strict provisions which will require immigration certificates. In fact, we favor every provision which tends to strengthen and safeguard entry and make impossible the admission of any individual immigrant who cannot in every way comply with every provision of the present stringent immigration laws. We are irrevocably opposed to the admission of even a single immigrant who is not physically, mentally, and morally fit eventually to become a real American citizen.

We do, however, protest against the reduction in the quota from 3 to 2 per cent, and especially against the per cent being based on the 1890 census in lieu of that of 1920 or 1910. We are of the opinion that it is a deliberate discrimination against the so-called newer immigration. If it was not intended to arbitrarily discriminate against the immigration from Austria, Czechoslovakia, Denmark, Italy, Norway, Poland, Rumania, Sweden, and other countries, why did the proponents of the measure take the 1890 census? It is too apparent that it is intended not to reduce immigration from Great Britain and Germany, but to completely estop almost all immigration from all of the other countries. At the time when the committee was considering the bill they had before them the actual figures showing what the result would be if the census of 1890 was adopted.

It certainly will not be contended by those who favor this measure that the reason for its adoption was a failure of display of loyalty and patriotism of those who came from southwestern Europe.

We realize that the committee cannot report a bill which would satisfy the two extremes, viz, first, those alarmists and extremists who at all times clamor even against the admission of the wives and children of our citizens and soldiers and who insist upon completely closing our doors to every immigrant, regardless how deserving and desirable; second, the class who for economical, personal, and financial advantages desire that the doors be opened not only to permit without limitation the entry of skilled but of all unskilled labor.

We feel that the adoption of the 1890 census is unjustifiable not only for the reason that it is discriminatory but because it will also prevent the admission of from sixty to seventy-five thousand laborers, who will shortly be greatly needed. We are not interested in supplying, as some may term, "cheap labor," but we are deeply concerned in the welfare of the United States, whose prosperity depends upon having at least a sufficient amount of unskilled labor. This can be obtained, in a measure, by using the population figures of 1920 or 1910 as a basis in lieu of the 1890 census as the majority has adopted. We doubt whether our northern and eastern unskilled labor requirements can be drawn from the south without at the same time injuring the growing southern industries. Surely, under the stringent provisions of the bill, no temporary common labor can be obtained from Mexico as was done in 1918 and 1919 to relieve the shortage of labor in the cotton and sugar-beet fields in the southern and southwestern states.

It cannot be truthfully denied that most of the hard, common, and manual work performed in the United States has been done during the past thirty and forty years by the immigrants coming from those countries designated as southern and southeastern Europe. Such work for the past century has always been performed by the then coming immigrants.

As has often been stated on the floor of the House and reiterated in the press of the country, the common understanding was that the present 3 per cent quota law was temporarily enacted for the sole purpose of safeguarding the United States against an anticipated influx of immigrants after the war. Since the enactment of the measure it was shown that many of the fears which were expressed were unfounded in fact, because several of the countries have not even made full use of their quotas. The 3 per cent quota law would have permitted the coming of over three hundred and fifty-five thousand immigrants, but approximately, in the last year, only three hundred and nine thousand, five hundred and fifty-six arrived. Further confirmation of our statement to the effect that those who would be coming would be mainly women and children is shown by the statement of Mr. Wixon, of the Bureau of Immigration, who testified before the Committee on Appropriations as follows:

That of the 309,556 immigrant aliens admitted during the first fiscal year, 95,846 of that number is represented by unmarried females and 31,980 represented by males under 16 years of age; or, in other words, nearly one-half of the entire number of immigrant aliens arriving is represented by what might be termed as dependent aliens, regarded strictly from an immigration standpoint. Something which surprised me more than anything else when statistics for the last fiscal year were compiled was the fact that our entire net gain in population is represented by 104,326 females and 6,518 males under 16 years of age. By that I mean that the figures given embrace the number of aliens arriving over those departing, and, as will be seen, we did not gain a single male over 16 years of age, the fact being that the number of males over that age departing was considerably in excess of the number arriving. It should be taken into consideration also that of males arriving a large number of them were over the age of 55 years and more or less dependent. In fact a great number of them were absolutely dependent.

The committee has also refused to make provision for the admission of domestics, admitted by all so greatly needed. We desire to call specific attention to a partial statement made by Mr. Augustine Davis, president of Davis Automatic Equipment Corporation, appearing in American Industries, entitled "Need more of the domestic class" (Hearings, 6-C):

The mothers in our own country generally find it next to impossible to obtain the aid necessary to care for their families properly.

The extreme difficulty in securing such assistance results in imperfect home sanitation, neglect of children, ill health and despondency in overworked mothers, unsatisfactory food preparation, lessens desire for home ownership, discourages marriage, increases unhealthy hotel and boarding-house life, tends to the disruption of families, leads to divorce, and is no small factor in "race suicide," all of which has a most detrimental effect on the morals and progress of our people.

Considerable stress has been laid by the proponents of

this measure that during the past two or three years immigration has consisted mainly of women and children. It must be borne in mind that during the entire war period, due to war conditions, it was impossible for husbands to bring over their wives and children. We believe that the highest morality can be attained, and for the best interest of home and country, that the wife and minor children should be under the same roof with the husband. We believe in the uniting of families; it brings peace and contentment; it helps to improve the home life in every community.

IMMIGRATION UNDER PERCENTUM LIMIT LAW[1]

Mr. Husband's review of the history of our immigration policy has brought to light certain important points. The first is that there has been at all times in our history a tendency on the part of some of those already here, not always a majority but at any rate a vocal and articulate minority, toward wishing to keep the country pure and unspotted from foreign or any outside contamination. He has also referred to the opposition to immigration before the Civil War. I have been making a study of the history of immigration during the past winter, and I have been amazed to find how threatening and how violent the opposition to the immigrant was at that time. Let us be thankful, however, that in the days of the rising tide of native Americanism, and during the period when the so-called Know-nothing movement ran its so-called "riotous career," some of our fathers stood firmly for what they believed to be the best interests of this country looking forward over a long period of time, and they refused to be stampeded into closing the gates of Castle Garden to the men who came from Europe,

[1] By Edith Abbott. National Conference of Social Work. Proceedings. 1922 : 463-6.

illiterate and poverty-stricken and oppressed as they were. Ask yourselves honestly what would have happened if we had adopted the narrow exclusionist policy that Australia and some of the other British commonwealths adopted. Has the Australian policy proved to be so much superior to the American policy? I do not believe you can honestly say that it has.

Immigration has always increased our domestic difficulties. No one wishes to deny that, but must we always sidestep the difficulties of life, or must we try to solve them? To admit strangers into your home, into your city, into your country makes life more difficult, but we can rise to face those difficulties if it is worth while. It is not and should not be the tradition of our country to follow or adopt one policy because it is the easy way and reject another because it is the hard way. To do that is to live in the un-American "gray twilight that knows neither victory nor defeat."

Now the method of dealing with immigration that this country adopted at a time when nearly two millions of starving Irish peasants were flocking to America as to the promised land, the method then adopted was not exclusion but protection, the provision by the states of such means of caring for these miserable and broken people as would make them good citizens instead of public burdens.

The founding in the year 1847 of the New York State Commissioners of Emigration—and by the way this was the first public welfare commission organized in the United States—the founding of this commission under the leadership of Thurlow Weed and some other public-spirited citizens of New York was the answer given in that day to the restrictionist argument. This act of 1847 and the succeeding act of 1848 were a benevolent gesture on the part of the state toward the poor, the friendless, and the ignorant who needed friends, advice, and protection in a new land.

Restriction of numbers on the quota basis is here to stay for the next two years. Can we not before the two years expire consider this subject with honesty and candor. To do this means raising the whole subject of regulation through an administrative commission and the probable repeal of the old contract labor law. If agreements approved by the Federal Trade Commission have been found to be a satisfactory protection against harmful agreements in one direction, cannot labor contracts be similarly approved or disapproved and put to rest the old idea that a contract entered into by an immigrant is necessarily harmful or dangerous instead of a protection to him or to the country.

Descending to the "gusty atmosphere of controversy" I wish to say in conclusion that it may be that we must come finally to accept as an accomplished fact that immigration will never again be open in this country to those who can show only sane minds, stout hearts, and strong hands and that they must show also long skulls and blue eyes or some evidence of belonging to that much glorified Nordic race. We are told that America is at last thinking of herself and not of Europe, but is selfishness so much more admirable in a nation than in an individual? If we must now think selfishly of our material gains do not let us forget to reckon our spiritual losses. Do we, the social workers of America, believe that a nation can live by bread alone? Do we think the greatest and richest nation in the world can live apart from the suffering people of Europe and into itself alone? Are we no longer our brother's keeper?

Whatever Congress may have voted, there are those of us left who believe that in closing the open door at the dictates of prejudice or thoughtlessness or greed or gain, we are sacrificing one of the noblest of our national traditions, an ideal expressed by James Russell Lowell in the Commemoration Ode which he read at the Harvard commencement after the Civil War in which he described our country as "her of the open heart and open door, with room about her hearth for all mankind." Immigration has always brought with it serious problems. We chose in the past to accept the harder part, to shoulder the responsibilities of absorbing a vast stream of new and strange people. It is a strange paradox that those who themselves came to this country only yesterday as it were, those who are only the second or third generation here, and the labor movement is full of them, should now so often assume the right to say that our country shall no longer provide "a shelter for the hunted head, for the starved laborer toil and bread." Is the open door, I ask you, to be closed forever by those who so recently were themselves reluctantly allowed to pass?

THE IMMIGRATION PROBLEM[1]

When the labor unions undertook to build up a great power throughout the country they were wise enough to recognize the fact that a shortage of unskilled labor is the greatest offensive weapon which they can possess. They realized that where there is a normal supply of unskilled labor the power of the union is not so effective because men want to keep their employment and are not so ready to obey the call of the leader who finds that his ability to penalize industry is increased commensurately with the shortage of workers. The first restriction imposed was the literacy test which was, and is, utterly unsound. This country has not reached its full development, and there are still necessary a tremendous number of workers to do the rough labor in connection with the industries and utilities. The literacy test shut out this type of labor to a large extent, and struck at the very root of our development because, unless the foundation work is done, the superstructure cannot be

[1] By William H. Barr, President of the Lumen Bearing Company and the National Founders Association. Metal Industry. February, 1923. p. 70.

completed. The unions were aided by the old cry that anarchists and communists were coming in too freely, but it was absolutely untrue as applied to illiterate workers. It was the men who could read, write, and orate who were the anarchists and communists, while the stolid well meaning laborer had no interest in that particular kind of propaganda.

Of course, the union success in forcing the literacy test naturally resulted in reaching out for other restrictions which would limit the amount of labor. Let it be remembered that there was no thought on the part of the unions that the workers who were coming in were either reducing wages or competing with American workers. That was a slogan offered to our people which no unionist leader ever believed. The result of the continuous agitation supported by people who believed that we were not assimilating the immigration that was coming in, resulted during 1917 in the 3 per cent law which is now on the statute books. It should be understood that it is not at all a net 3 per cent law in the sense that such a quota is added to our workers every year because emigration is debited against immigration, and in some cases almost offsets it.

We have, therefore, the literacy test which is utterly stupid, and the 3 per cent restrictive limitation which has succeeded in merely steadily decreasing the number of workers available and particularly at this time when the country is beginning to forge ahead out of the slough of post-war depression. There can be no real prosperity, no definite industrial expansion unless there is a sufficient supply of unskilled labor. No one will assert that we have reached today a full measure of prosperity or that our expansion has nearly reached the possibilities which should follow our recent depression. But on the verge of such an advance we find a shortage of all kinds of labor, which will act as the most effective brake that it is possible to conceive. If we are willing to concede increased power to the labor unions with which they may further limit the return of our possible prosperity then, of course, we are heading for economic disaster.

The existing shortage of labor due to the restrictive immigration laws will inevitably result in demands for higher wages and will bring about lessened efficiency. There can be no question as to the certainty of these things and it is equally certain the cost of commodities will correspondingly rise and we shall have an even greater problem in the high cost of living. It will not be merely increased wages which will produce this increased cost in living, but decreased efficiency together with the lack of sufficient labor will produce an economic condition, inevitably causing higher prices and decreased prosperity. Any increase in prices for goods is likely to result in another buyers' strike, such as we experienced not so long ago, and a buyers' strike will surely check prosperity. This is not presenting a theory, but submitting inevitable hard facts. Let those who would dispute such deductions produce any evidence to the contrary, or show by any form of legislation how such a condition can be avoided. Take the immigration problem out of politics, put it in the hands of scientifically trained men and let us have economic laws without the intervention of artificial influences by favored classes who seek their own betterment at the expense of the nation's industries and the nation's prosperity.

A CONSTRUCTIVE IMMIGRATION POLICY [1]

Agriculture and industry are equally interested in the social and economic problem of immigration. Each is feeling in an increasing degree a rising demand for labor to which, with a single exception, there has been substantially no foreign contribution in six years. Yet,

[1] By James A. Emery, General Counsel of the National Association of Manufacturers. American Industries. January, 1923. p. 9-10.

neither agriculture nor industry desire to satisfy economic requirements at the expense of quality in citizenship. The problem, then, is to practically apply the rule laid down by James Madison in his famous report on immigration to the First Congress: "Welcome every person of good fame that really means to incorporate himself into our society, but repel all who will not be a real addition to the wealth and strength of the United States."

We are a nation of immigrants and the descendants of immigrants. Mere prejudice against the man of foreign blood sits ill upon us, but it is equally true that we have learned that unassimilated immigration threatens national indigestion. We have established reliance upon immigration as the great source of supply for rough and unskilled labor, without which the basic work of expanding construction, transportation, manufacture and agriculture cannot go forward, we therefore have an economic need and must undertake to determine how to meet it without prejudice, and in the light of ascertained facts, but with a firm determination to admit only those mentally and physically sound, capable of citizenship and subject to control, during their alienage, by Federal authority, and receiving reliable information as to opportunities and education toward citizenship through private and public cooperation.

What, then, are the facts about our immigration; what is its nature and amount; how are we presently undertaking to regulate it, and, if our present method is unsatisfactory, what constructive suggestion is to be made that may at once help us to meet economic necessities while protecting the quality of our blood and citizenship in the national interest?

Within a hundred years we have admitted to the United States some thirty-four and three-quarter millions of immigrants. Until 1890, the great portion of this foreign stream flowed from the Nordic countries and represented the strains which experience demonstrated to most readily accept our ideals and institutions, and adapt themselves to our customs and traditions and mode of life. During the next twenty-five years that preceded the great war, the Slavic and southern countries of Europe increased their immigration flow to a very considerable extent. Economically, the industrial, agricultural, transportation and mining development of the nation moved forward in continuing dependence upon an immigrant stream of willing laborers performing the rougher tasks which the native-born declined or were insufficient in number to meet.

The extent of this dependence is illustrated by an average annual immigration from 1909 to 1914 of substantially nine hundred and twenty-five thousand. Of this, the average annual number of skilled laborers was in excess of one hundred and fifteen thousand, common laborers more than twenty-two thousand, and farmers and farm laborers averaged over two hundred and fifty thousand.

From 1915 to 1919, immigration was abruptly suspended by the great world catastrophe. During 1920-1921, it again reached about six hundred and sixty-eight thousand. Alarmed by the well-founded fear that we were confronted with a serious invasion of undesirable aliens and unable to devise for the moment a constructive means to meet it, the Congress enacted, in 1920, a 3 per cent limitation, which was pocket vetoed by President Wilson but eventually reenacted in May, 1921.

This proposal was not a substitute for the Act of February, 1917, but restricted the otherwise admissible aliens who might enter under it to 3 per cent of the number of foreign-born persons of each nationality resident in the United States, as evidenced by the Census of 1910. Not more than 20 per cent of such annual quota are admissible in any one month. For the purpose of the act, nationality is determined by the country of birth. Thus a white person born in Africa becomes an African, and for that reason white persons have been rejected because the African quota was filled. The restrictive provisions do not apply to the countries of the North American continent, but nevertheless include with the Asiatic barred zones substantially 75 per cent of the earth's surface.

Thus, under the first year of the operation of this restriction, 356,995 aliens were admissible to the United States, of which number but 243,953 were admitted. The restrictive act does not, however, take into account in balancing its quotas the continuing flow of emigration. Thus, while many of the northern European countries have not filled their quota, and most of the southern European countries have, the net immigration is in favor of Germany, the United Kingdom, Mexico, Scandinavia and France, while Poland, Italy, Spain, the Balkan countries, Portugal and Lithuania had emigration in excess of immigration.

It thus becomes inevitable that, given substantially six years with little or no immigration and one year of severe restriction, we face an enormous diminution of our customary labor supply, reflecting itself throughout industry, transportation, construction and agriculture. The first fiscal year of the operation of the 3 per cent act leaves us with a net gain of male immigrant aliens admitted over male emigrant aliens departed, of but 6,518.

These facts are themselves the overwhelming evidence of a shortage in industrial and agricultural labor that must be steadily intensified and which, if unrelieved, must necessarily have the most serious economic effects.

The present Act penalizes any form of solicitation, inducement or encouragement of immigration except that skilled labor may be sought outside the country in individual cases, with the approval of the Secretary of Labor, upon proof that labor unemployed, cannot be found in this country. The provision offers no relief for the present shortage of unskilled labor and no procedure by which the administrative remedy can be provided, however overwhelming the proof that immediate alleviation could be afforded by permitting the admission of otherwise admissible aliens in excess of quotas, where the shortage can be demonstrated. Such relief, surrounded with appropriate safeguards, is immediately required. If such desirable and practical aid is not now permitted, the farms will suffer a still further shortage through the higher inducements of industrial labor, the cost of foodstuffs will increase because of contracted production and increasing expense, while skilled labor will suffer lessened opportunity for employment because of the shortage of indispensable preliminary labor to prepare basic materials and perform fundamental operations before craftsmen may apply their skill. The whole country will be affected by the situation if it is unrelieved, for steadily rising costs are inevitable in every field for employment, but particularly in agriculture and industry.

However vital the relief suggested, it is but a necessary makeshift. The time has come when the American people should turn their attention to the formulation of a constructive policy of selective immigration and abandon the present negative legislation which neither permits the satisfaction of economic requirements indispensable to national development or the effective control, education and distribution of the alien during the period of his alienage, or the application of practical tests for admission where immigration originates.

The time is too short for exhaustive discussion, but reason and experience are suggesting the means by which Madison's fundamental formula may be given practical application. Is it not worth while to consider an immigration policy that will:

I. Distinguish between requirements for admission and naturalization, applying the tests for the former through our own officers at the point where passports are viséd or at least at the point of debarkation. The tests of admission to exclude, as we do now, the diseased, the defectives, the criminal, the enemies of all countries and of this government, but abandoning a literacy test vetoed by three Presidents, which the Lenins and Trotskys of the world pass with ease, and which are mere evidence of original handicaps and are neither mental or moral tests of capacity for citizenship. Had they been applied to the ancestors of our most useful and illustrious citizens, we should never have heard most of their names.

2. The United States should assert the right to register, supervise, educate and distribute the alien during the period of his alienage and to administer its law through a board, including the secretaries of Labor, Commerce and Agriculture, thus assuring a coordination of the departments most vitally interested and most widely and accurately informed respecting the economic requirements and opportunities of the United States. Emphasizing the importance of the problem and securing the cooperation of the states and private organization, such a plan would assure the compilation and analysis of the most accurate information continually renewed. It would guide a broad, sympathetic, informed policy, assuring at once a scientific and systematic assembly of national needs, generous consideration for the opportunities of the alien and effective protection of the national interest through the admission of those capable of citizenship, and their preparation for induction into it under uniform Federal law.

But, important as is the adoption of a constructive policy of selective immigration, the nation, starved of its customary labor for more than five years, needs now immediate relief that will meet demonstrated economic necessity while maintaining the existing safeguards against undesirable aliens.

To this end, Congress ought at once to modify the existing act by:

1. Permitting ascertained emigration to be charged against ascertained immigration in determining national quotas.

2. Authorizing the Secretary of Labor to admit otherwise admissible and desirable labor in excess of quotas where the necessity for such labor is clearly demonstrated and it is not obtainable in this country.

3. Authorizing the Secretary of Labor, in conjunction with other appropriate officials, to immediately provide, as far as practicable, for the determination of the admissibility of aliens at the point where their passports are viséd, or at least at the chief port of debarkation.

INCREASED IMMIGRATION NEEDED [1]

Most of the current arguments in favor of increased immigration are based on the "labor shortage" theory. We need more aliens to do the heavy work, it is said, Joseph F. Doherty writes in Trade Winds, published by the Union Trust Co. of Cleveland:

What it means to American enterprise, if the losses in unskilled labor through remigration, death and other causes, cannot be replaced, is indicated by certain well-established facts concerning the relationship of our foreign born workers and those of foreign parentage to American industry. The workers of foreign birth and parentage represent one-third of the people of the United States, yet they mine three-fourths of the coal, manufacture three-fourths of the clothing, half of the silk, linen, wool, lace and embroidered goods; bake more than half of the bread, refine more than half of the sugar, and put up half of the canned goods. They have built our railroads with the aid of American capital and still do half of the maintenance work on the railroads and the streets. Half of the work in the blast furnaces, in the carpet mills, hemp and jute factories, and the copper, silver, brass, gold, rubber, and leather goods is done by the foreign born and their descendants.

We rarely consider these facts in our discussions of national policies on immigration, nor do we, as a rule, take into account the fact that the foreign born are of great importance economically; that they constitute part of the warp and woof of the commercial fabric of the country. It is estimated that the

[1] From Industrial Digest. February, 1923. p. 146.

real estate holdings of Italians in New York city amount to $100,000,000. In Cleveland, where the volume of retail business is estimated at more than $20,000,000 annually, more than 50 per cent of the dealers are foreign born. In Minnesota, the State Auditor's office reported that two-thirds of the farm stock and equipment of that state is owned by Swedes and Norwegians, by birth and descent, and represents $666,000,000.

Since immigrants started to come to America in large numbers, the wealth of the nation has grown from less than ten billion dollars to over one hundred billion, the number of wage earners has increased seven times; wages have increased twenty times and the value of products has grown from one billion to twenty-five billions of dollars. Since the immigrants made possible the present-day expansion of industry, are we to interpret the existing attitude and policy on immigration as an admission that America has reached the peak of her development and that we cannot go a step beyond?

Magnus W. Alexander, managing director of the National Industrial Conference Board, thus presents the economic advantages of the immigrant, in the Engineering News-Record:

The fact is generally recognized that the industries of the United States have been built up in a large measure through the immigrant labor supply. The foreign born male in the United States is essentially here to work. The 1920 census shows that in general 89 per cent of all male foreign born whites, ten years of age and over, in the United States, are gainfully employed; in the New England and Middle Atlantic States 91 per cent of them are gainfully employed. This is in contrast with a general average of 75 per cent of the native whites so employed and 81 per cent of the negroes. In agriculture the foreign born are almost negligible, but in the mining industry they represent 35 per cent of all those gainfully employed. In the manufacturing and mechanical industries 28 per cent of those gainfully employed are foreign born and 23 per cent more are of foreign or mixed parentage. Of all foreign-born workers in the United States 47 per cent are employed in the manufacturing and mechanical industries.

The fact that immigrant labor constitutes a fluid supply that comes when it is wanted and departs when labor conditions are unfavorable, makes it economically advantageous. Moreover the immigrants arrive predominantly at the working age. The census figures of 1890, 1900 and 1910 show that about 85 per cent of the foreign born are in the age groups of sixteen to sixty-four, which is the predominant working span.

There is, unquestionably, a shortage of common labor and there will be a much greater shortage this summer, especially in the steel industry. Some countries are not sending us as many persons as are admissible under the law. Moreover, we find that many laborers have emigrated. Apparently conditions in this country are not sufficiently attractive to people whom our industries desire and need.

Many people are, however, willing to let as many aliens come in as want to, providing they are desirable, and are willing to become American citizens, and providing they do not come in such large numbers as to upset very abruptly any existing relationship.

The principal difficulty regarding immigration is that no means exists at the present time for determining the immigration needs of the country. The first step to be taken in solving the immigration problem is to appoint a fact-finding commission that will endeavor to secure information upon which immigration legislation can be based, to best serve the needs of the United States.—*S. R. Rectanus, Director, Personnel Service, The American Rolling Mill Company.*

It seems to me that a continuation of the present condition is going to operate as a hardship on both employers and employees. Since those employers who need this class of labor will be unable to operate to full capacity, the law may have a tendency to prevent the advancement of those, who are at present doing common labor, to the higher skilled positions.

In the past the advancement of foreign labor to the higher skilled positions has been in a great many instances very rapid and it is absolutely essential that there shall be an ample supply of labor coming to this country at all times to fill the positions of lower rank that are left vacant by those who are advanced to the occupations of greater skill.—*J. M. Larkin, Assistant to the President of the Bethlehem Steel Company.*

The law passed by Congress soon after the war restricting immigration is wholly responsible for the present labor shortage. If this law had never gone on the statute books, if our portals had remained as free to immigration since the war as they were before the war and as they have been throughout our history, our inflated wage scale would have been well liquidated before now.

That wages would not deflate when there was a shortage of labor should have been clear to the Washington statesmen. It should have been clear to them because of the fact that America does not produce its own labor, and never has produced its own labor since the formation of the government. Our only domestic labor outside of the rural sections is colored, and in the north that is wholly negligible. There isn't enough of it to make a dent in the situation.

We must have a substratum of plain labor. Modern life and modern civilization cannot exist without it. Any change in the immigration law that would let into this country more plain labor and more skilled mechanics will be fought to the limit by organized labor. Whether our present restrictive law was passed at the behest of organized labor I do not know; but I do know that the law is exactly what organized labor has been contending for, and what organized labor will contend for with all its force.—*Frank A. Munsey, in address before the American Bankers Association, October* 4, 1922.

Not the least indication of the upward trend of business is the present employment situation. Employment is always an indication of the business pulse of a nation. Already we are beginning to feel a pinch in labor supply. This is essentially true of unskilled labor. That pinch, perhaps, will not be relieved until the laws for the restriction of immigration are loosened. Judging by industrial conditions, one reasonably could say that our immigration laws have gone too far in barring the immigrant who is needed here and who needs us. Every impediment should be placed before the type of immigrant who cannot make a contribution toward the growth of the nation and accept the just reward for his labor, but, at the same time, there should be encouragement for him that will. Men and women who qualify mentally, morally and physically for entry into this country should not be debarred by percentage rulings. These people have something definite to offer the country, their strength and their allegiance; the country has something definite to offer them, economic freedom and citizenship. Each needs the other for mutual benefit.

As the men step up from the lower places in the industrial ranks their places are left vacant. Unfortunately industry cannot move without the power of those who have nothing but their muscles to offer. They form an important and integral part in making the wheels go round. The country will always need them. Our only source of supply is the immigrant who has not yet had the opportunity to take his place among more highly skilled labor. To close our door to him is to do injury to ourselves. There should always be enough additional labor to take care of the industrial growth of the country. One cannot make hard and fast rules about this; one must apply wisdom and judgment as the need arises.

—*Elbert H. Gary in New York Times.*

It is natural and commendable that the man who is working at common labor fit himself for occupations requiring a greater degree of skill and which are correspondingly better compensated. But unless we can find labor to take the places of ambitious workers they cannot rise from more common occupations. The ranks of skilled and semi-skilled occupations are fast being filled —the professional and clerical classes are overcrowded —and the labor market is becoming top heavy because there are not enough workers to take care of the raw material and fashion it into shape so it can be passed along to the better skilled mechanics and artisans. Industry will stop unless an unfailing supply of common labor is obtainable from abroad. We have always secured our bulk of labor from the muscular races overseas; it is to their advantage to come to this country and it is to the advantage of all our people, including our workers who would progress, that they be permitted to immigrate in numbers sufficient to supply the labor deficiency.—*William Butterworth, President, Deere and Company.*

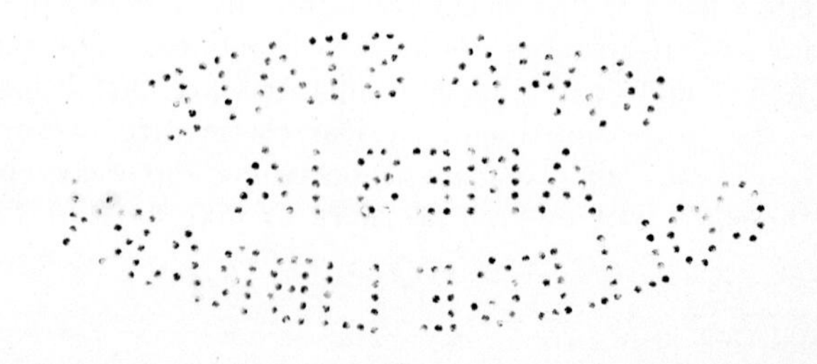